® teach yourself

word 2007

moira stephen

for over 60 years, more than 50 million people have learnt over 750 subjects the **teach yourself** way, with impressive results.

be where you want to be with **teach yourself**

For UK order enquiries: please contact Bookpoint Ltd, 130 Milton Park, Abingdon, Oxon OX14 4SB. Telephone: +44 (0)1235 827720. Fax: +44 (0)1235 400454. Lines are open 09.00–17.00, Monday to Saturday, with a 24-hour message answering service. Details about our titles and how to order are available at www.teachyourself.co.uk.

For USA order enquiries: please contact McGraw-Hill Customer Services, PO Box 545, Blacklick, OH 43004-0545, USA. Telephone: 1-800-722-4726. Fax: 1-614-755-5645.

For Canada order enquiries: please contact McGraw-Hill Ryerson Ltd, 300 Water St, Whitby, Ontario L1N 9B6, Canada. Telephone: 905 430 5000. Fax: 905 430 5020.

Long renowned as the authoritative source for self-guided learning – with more than 50 million copies sold worldwide – the **teach yourself** series includes over 500 titles in the fields of languages, crafts, hobbies, business, computing and education.

British Library Cataloguing in Publication Data: a catalogue record for this title is available from The British Library.

Library of Congress Catalog Card Number: on file.

First published in UK 2007 by Hodder Education, 338 Euston Road, London NW1 3BH.

First published in USA 2007 by The McGraw-Hill Companies Inc.

The **teach yourself** name is a registered trademark of Hodder Headline.

Computer hardware and software brand names mentioned in this book are protected by their respective trademarks and are acknowledged.

The publisher has used its best endeavours to ensure that the URLs for external websites referred to in this book are correct and active at the time of going to press. However, the publisher has no responsibility for the websites and can give no guarantee that a site will remain live or that the content is or will remain appropriate.

 Typeset by MacDesign, Southampton

Printed in Great Britain for Hodder Education, a division of Hodder Headline, 338 Euston Road, London NW1 3BH, by Cox & Wyman Ltd, Reading, Berkshire.

Hodder Headline's policy is to use papers that are natural, renewable and recyclable products and made from wood grown in sustainable forests. The logging and manufacturing processes are expected to conform to the environmental regulations of the country of origin.

Impression number   10 9 8 7 6 5 4 3 2 1

Year   2011 2010 2009 2008 2007

contents

preface

Welcome to *Teach Yourself Word*.

If you need to produce letters, reports, minutes, manuals, lists, newsletters, posters, forms, CVs, invitations or brochures you'll find all the features you require in Word. This book will help you unleash the power of Word, quickly and painlessly. We start by introducing the basic skills that are required to create and format a document attractively. We then look at some of the tools that can improve your efficiency and productivity when using the package – tools that help automate tasks, e.g. AutoText, styles and templates.

The power and flexibility of tables are demonstrated by showing how they can be used in a variety of situations from simple table layout through to forms design. You'll also find out how to perform basic calculations within tables and produce graphs to display the table data.

If you work with long documents, you'll love the features that make handling them easy, e.g. headers and footers, table of contents, indexing, outline and master document view, footnotes, endnotes, bookmarks, etc.

Other features covered include templates, mail merge, clip art, WordArt, macros, integration with other Office applications, and using Word to send e-mail.

Word is a very powerful word processing package – but don't let that put you off – you'll be amazed at what can be achieved relatively easily! I hope you enjoy using this book and find it useful when learning to use Word.

Moira Stephen
2007

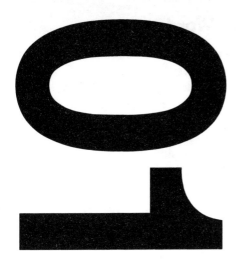

01

getting started

In this chapter you will learn:

- what you need to run Word 2007
- how to install the software
- how to start Word
- about the Word screen and its tools
- how to use the Help system

1.1 Introducing Word

Word is a very powerful word processor – but don't let that put you off! It can be used to create simple letters, memos and reports – and you'll soon discover how easy it is to generate these. You can use the more sophisticated features in Word to produce mail shots, forms, newsletters and multi-page publications. Word integrates well with other packages in the Microsoft Office suite, which will help you create professional documents that combine files generated in other applications. Finally, if you have Internet access, you'll learn how to hyperlink to documents and Internet addresses, send e-mails and publish content to your blog!

It is assumed that you have a working knowledge of Windows.

1.2 System requirements

The hardware and software specifications given are for Office 2007. The recommended configuration is a PC with a minimum of a 500 MHz processor, 256 MB of RAM and 1.5 GB disk space. The minimum specification is given in the table below.

Processor	500 MHz or higher
Memory	256 MB RAM or higher
Hard disk	1.5 GB. A portion of this will be freed after installation if the installation files are removed from the hard drive.
Drive	CD-ROM or DVD drive
Display	1024 × 768 pixels or higher resolution monitor
Operating system	Windows XP with Service Pack 2, Windows Server with Service Pack 1, or later system
Other	Certain features, e.g. inking, speech recognition, Information Rights Management have specific requirements – check out the Microsoft website.
Browser	Internet Explorer 6.0 or later, 32-bit browser only.

See http://www.microsoft.com for full details of system requirements.

Word is present in all of the Office 2007 suite editions. For full details of what is included in each edition visit http://www.microsoft.com.

1.3 Installing Word

To install Microsoft Office, follow the on-screen instructions:

1 Insert the Microsoft Office CD into the CD drive.

♦ The CD will launch automatically, and the setup will begin.

2 At the Setup dialog box, enter the 25-character product key.

3 For the user information, enter your name, initials (optional) and organization (optional).

♦ Your name will be used in the Author box in the Properties dialog box in the Office programs.

4 Read the End-User License Agreement and select 'I accept the terms' (if you don't agree, you can't continue).

5 Select the type of installation you require.

6 At the final Setup stage, select the options and you're done!

Entering your product key at installation helps to verify that your software is legitimate. You will be able to run your 2007 Microsoft Office system programs up to 25 times before you have to enter a product key – after this time the software goes into Reduced Functionality mode and many features will be unavailable.

1.4 Starting Word

1 Click the **Start** button on the Taskbar.

2 Point to **All Programs**.

3 Select **Microsoft Office**.

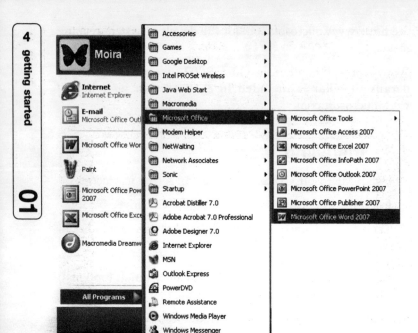

4   Click Microsoft Office Word 2007.

1.5 The Word screen

When Word starts, you are presented with a new blank document so you can just start typing in your text.

We'll take a tour of the Word screen, so that you know what the various areas are called. You'll find the screen areas referred to by their proper names in the online Help, throughout this book and in other publications on the package.

If the document window is maximized, the file and the Application windows share one title bar containing the application and document names (e.g. *Document1*).

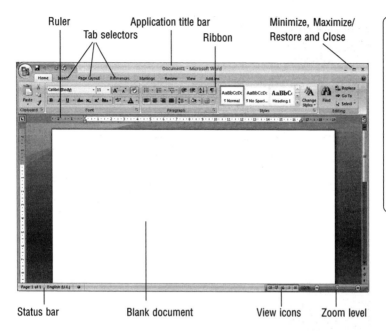

| Ruler | | Application title bar | | Minimize, Maximize/ |
| Tab selectors | | | Ribbon | Restore and Close |

Status bar   Blank document   View icons   Zoom level

1.6 Ribbon and tabs

Word features and commands are displayed along the top of the work area in a section of the screen called the Ribbon. This is divided into task-orientated Tabs, where the commands and features required to perform different tasks are grouped together, e.g. the Insert tab has all the objects you might want to insert.

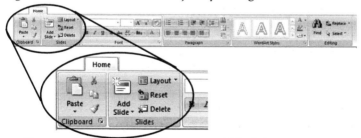

• You can hide the ribbon by pressing **[Ctrl]-[F1]**.

• Click any tab to display it again, or press **[Ctrl][F1]**.

Program tabs replace the standard tabs when you perform certain tasks, e.g. Print Preview.

Groups and command buttons

The command buttons on each tab are arranged in groups, e.g. the Insert tab has all the buttons grouped together into areas – shapes, pages, tables, illustrations, links, header & footer, text and symbols.

The Microsoft Office button

The Microsoft Office button is located at the top left of the Word screen. When clicked it displays a menu that gives you access to all the things you can do with your file, e.g. print, save, open, send.

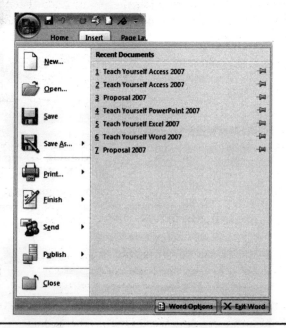

1.7 Quick Access toolbar

The Quick Access toolbar contains commands that are used regularly, and are independent from the tab being displayed. The toolbar can be displayed in one of two positions:

- Above the Ribbon, beside the Microsoft Office button (default position).
- Below the Ribbon.

To move it from one position to the other:

1 Click the down arrow at the right of the Quick Access toolbar.

2 Click **Place Quick Access Toolbar below the Ribbon** or **Place Quick Access Toolbar above the Ribbon** as required.

Customizing the Quick Access toolbar

You may find it useful to add other commands that you use regularly to this toolbar, e.g. open file, new file. You can easily add or remove tools.

To add a command:

1 Right-click on the command that you want to add.

2 Left-click on **Add to Quick Access Toolbar...**

To remove a command:

1 Right-click on the command that you wish to remove.

2 Left-click on **Remove from Quick Access Toolbar**.

If you have several buttons to add or remove from the toolbar, you could do so from the Word Options dialog box.

To display the Customize options:

1 Right-click on the Microsoft Office button.

2 Left-click on **Customize Quick Access Toolbar...**

3 Explore the Word Options, Customize area and add or re-move tools as required.

To add a command:

4 Select it in the list on the left.

5 Click **Add>>**.

To remove a command:

6 Select it in the list on the right.

7 Click **Remove**.

To change the position of the commands on the toolbar:

8 Select a command in the list on the right.

9 Click the up or down arrow to the right of this list.

To reset the toolbar to its original settings:

10 Click **Reset** at the bottom of the right-hand list.

11 Confirm that this is what you want to do at the prompt.

12 Click **OK**.

Dialog box launchers

Dialog box launchers are small buttons that appear at the bottom right of some groups. Clicking the launcher opens a dialog box that displays more options related to the group.

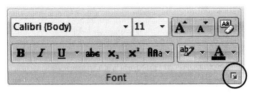

1.8 Ribbon keyboard shortcuts

If you prefer to issue commands using the keyboard, Word will automatically prompt you as you work.

1 Hold down [**Alt**] – and keep it down throughout the procedure.

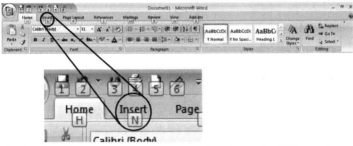

2 A ghost letter appears next to each tab on the Ribbon. Press the letter on your keyboard to activate the tab you want.

◆ Ghost letters/numbers will appear next to each command.

3 Press the letter/number to select the command required.

4 Release [**Alt**].

1.9 Status bar configuration

The Status bar contains several status indicators to help you as you work with your file.

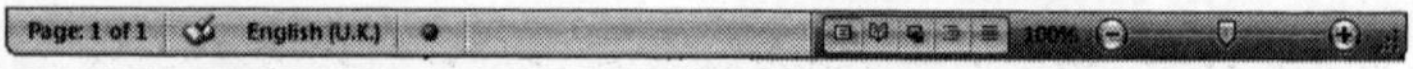

You can add and remove these indicators so that you display those that you find most useful.

To edit the indicators:

1 Right-click anywhere on the Status bar.

2 Select or deselect the indicator in the Status Bar Configuration menu.

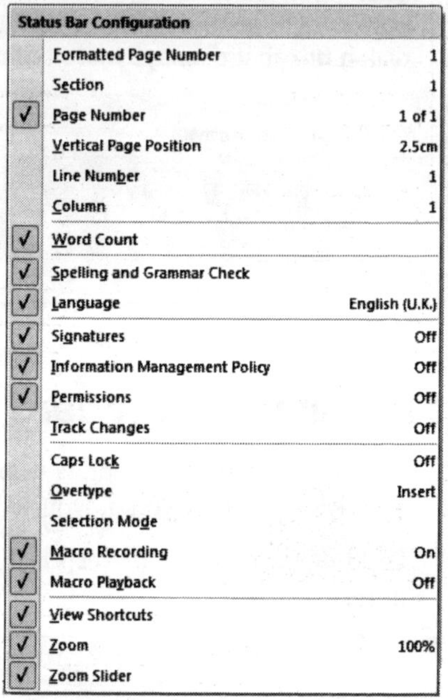

1.10 Help

As you work with Word you will most probably find that you come a bit unstuck from time to time and need help. If you are off-line, Word will use the Help system installed locally, if you are on-line you will have access to all the Help on the Microsoft website too.

To access the Help system:

1 Click the **Help** button to the right of the Ribbon.

Or

2 Press [F1].

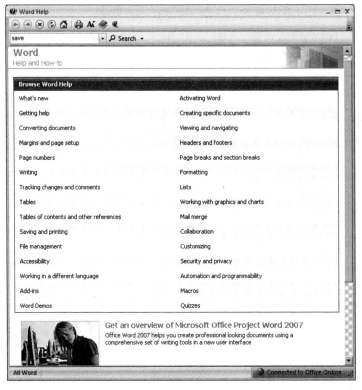

- If you are used to using Word, but are new to 2007, check out the *What's New* area.

- If you are new to Word, try *Getting Help* so that you can check out different places to look for Help.

- You could also try the *Word Demos* – or just have a browse through anything that looks interesting!

The Help toolbar

Use the Help toolbar as you work in the Help pages.

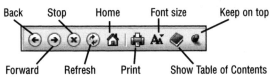

- **Back** – takes you back to the previous Help page visited.

- **Forward** – if you have used Back to go back, you can use Forward to move forward through the pages again.

- **Stop** – stops downloading a Help page. If you change your mind, or a page is slow to come in you might want to stop it.

- **Refresh** – updates the current page.

- **Home** – returns you to the Home page of the Help system.

- **Print** – prints out the current Help page.

- **Change Font Size** – increases or decreases the size of font.

- **Show/hide Table of Contents** – displays the contents list. You can browse through this to get an overview of what you can do with Word. To open or close a book (topic), click on it. This will expand the book to display other books or pages. When you click on a page it is displayed on the right.

- **Keep on top/Not on top** – controls whether or not the Help page stays on top of the Word window. If you are following instructions in the Help system to carry out a task, being able to keep the window visible is useful.

Searching for Help

If you know what you want Help on, you can search for it.

1 Enter details of what you are looking for in the **Search** field.

2 Click **Search** to search all the available Help sources.

Or

3 Click the Search arrow to drop down the menu and select an area in which to look.

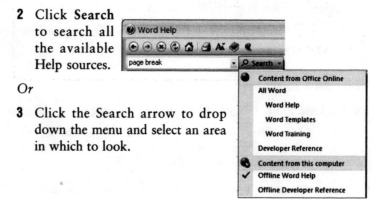

1.11 Exiting Word

When you have finished working in Word you must close the application down – don't just switch off your computer.

To exit Word:

1 Click the Microsoft Office button.

2 Click **Exit Word** at the bottom right of the menu.

Or

* Click the **Close** button in the top right-hand corner of the application title bar.

Summary

This chapter has introduced you to Word 2007. We have discussed:

* The minimum software and hardware requirements
* The installation procedure
* Accessing the package using the Start menu
* The Word screen
* The Ribbon and its tabs
* The Quick Access toolbar
* Choosing commands using the keyboard
* Status bar configuration
* The Help system
* Exiting Word.

02 basic Word skills

In this chapter you will learn:

- how to create, save, print, open and close documents
- entering and editing text
- how to move and copy text
- about proofing documents
- about viewing options

2.1 File handling

What follows is a summary of the main file handling features you will use when working with Word – create new, open, save, save as and close. All of these commands are found in the menu that is displayed when you click the Microsoft Office button.

When you start Word, a new document is created automatically – all that you need to do is type in your text. The document name, *Document1*, is displayed on the document title bar. Each new document created during a session in Word is given a name following the same format. The second will be called *Document2*, and so on. These names should be considered temporary – when you save your document, give it a new, meaningful name. You can create a new blank document at any time.

To create a new blank document:

1 Click the Microsoft Office button, and then click **New...**

2 At the **New Document** dialog box, in the **Blank and recent** category, select *Blank document*.

3 Click **Create**.

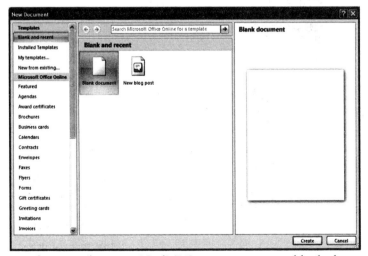

- Alternatively, press [Ctrl]-[N] to create a new blank document without opening the dialog box.

Open a document

To open an existing document:

1 Click the Microsoft Office button, then click **Open...**

2 Locate and select the document in the **Open** dialog box.

3 Click **Open**.

Or

♦ Press [Ctrl]-[O] to display the **Open** dialog box.

Recently-used files are listed on the right of the menu – to open one, click on its name in the Recent Documents list

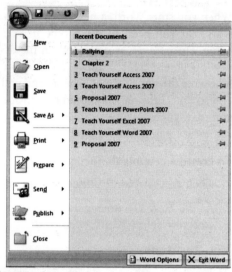

Save a document

At some stage you must save your file (if you don't you will lose it when you exit Word). When you save your document, you should give it a filename that reflects its contents rather than use the *Document1* temporary name.

The first time that you save your file it doesn't matter whether you use Save or Save As – both will take you to the Save As dialog box.

Save As...

1 Click the Microsoft Office button, then click **Save As...**

2 At the **Save As** dialog box, locate the folder into which to save your document (usually *My Documents* or a subfolder).

3 Enter the name in the **File name:** field.

4 Leave the **Save as type:** at *Word document*.

5 Click **Save**.

You are returned to your document. The name appears on the title bar.

◆ The keyboard shortcut for **Save As...** is [**F12**].

You can save your document at any time – you don't need to wait until you've entered all your text. I suggest you save your file regularly, and remember to resave it when you make changes to it. If your computer crashes or you have a power failure, you may lose any unsaved data.

Save

Once the document has been saved you can save your changes to it whenever you wish.

◆ Click **Save** on the Quick Access toolbar.

Or

◆ Click the Microsoft Office button, then **Save**.

The Save As dialog box does not reappear, but the up-to-date version of the file replaces the old one already saved to disk.

◆ Alternatively, press [**Ctrl**]-[**S**] to save your document.

Save As a different file

There may be times that you save a document, edit it, then decide that you want to save the edited version of the file and keep the original version too. If you don't want to overwrite the original with the updated version, click the Microsoft Office button and choose Save As... so you can select a different folder and/or filename for the new version of the file.

Password protection

If you wish to password protect your document (so that no one can open or edit the file unless they know the password) you can do so from the Save As dialog box.

1 Click the **Tools** button at the bottom left of the dialog box.

2 Choose **General Options...**

3 Enter the password(s) and click **OK**.

4 Re-enter the password(s) at the prompt and click **OK** again.

Close document

♦ Click the Microsoft Office button, then click **Close**.

Or

♦ Click the **Close** button on the title bar.

2.2 Entering text

When you open Word, or create a new blank document, you are given a blank page with the insertion point – a flashing black vertical bar – at the top left of the text area on the first page. All you have to do is type! Your text will appear at the insertion point. Try entering something – you could copy the text below.

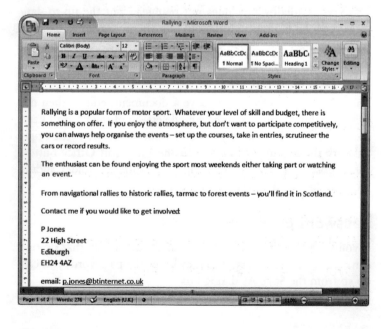

Remember to save your file if you want to keep it.

Things to remember when entering text into your document:

- DO NOT press [Enter] at the end of each line of text. If a sentence is going to run onto a new line, let it – the text will be wrapped automatically at the end of the line.

- DO press [Enter] at the end of a paragraph – Word will automatically leave some space between one paragraph and the next (10 pt initially).

- To force a new line without making a new paragraph, e.g. in between the lines in an address, hold down the [Shift] key and press [Enter].

2.3 Moving around your document

Once you have entered some text, you must be able to move around it and reposition the insertion point anywhere within your file. There are various ways of moving the insertion point – the most commonly used ones are discussed here. Experiment with them, then use whatever method suits you best!

Using the mouse:

1 Position the I-beam (the pointer when over a text area) where you want to move the insertion point to.

2 Click the left button.

Using the keyboard:

To move a character or line at a time:

- Press the right, left, up or down arrow (cursor) keys until the insertion point is where you want it.

To move right or left a word at a time:

- Hold down [Ctrl] and press the right or left arrow key.

To move up or down a paragraph at a time:

- Hold down [Ctrl] and press the up or down arrow key.

Other useful ones – to move:

• [End] to go to *the end of the line* that the insertion point is on.

• [Home] to go to *the start of the line* the insertion point is in.

• [Ctrl]-[Home] to move to *the start of the document*.

• [Ctrl]-[End] to move to *the end of the document*.

2.4 Basic editing techniques

Once you have started typing up your document, you will certainly want to edit it in some way. It may be because you have made a typing error, or because you have changed your mind about what you want to say.

When editing, you can insert new text, or delete or type over and replace existing text.

To insert text:

1 Position the insertion point where you want to add text.

2 Type in the new text.

To delete text:

1 Position the insertion point next to the character that you want to delete.

• If the insertion point is to the *right* of the character, press the backspace key [←] once for each character.

• If the insertion point is to the *left*, press [Delete] once for each character.

Both [←] and [Delete] repeat – if you hold them down they will zoom through your text removing it much quicker than you could type it in, so be careful with them!

Overtype

If you try to insert text, and notice that it is replacing text that is already there, you are in Overtype mode. Overtype mode is not activated initially in this version of Word – if it is on, someone has switched it on.

If Overtype is activated, it can be switched off and on by pressing **[Insert]** – and as [Insert] is usually next to [Delete] it can be very easy to go into Overtype mode by accident. You can turn off the key's ability to toggle the mode.

To activate Overtype mode:

1 Click the Microsoft Office button, then click **Word Options**.

2 Choose **Advanced**.

3 Select or deselect the Overtype options as required.

4 Click **OK**.

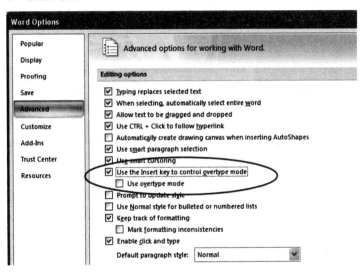

2.5 Spelling and grammar

To help you produce accurate work, Word can check the spelling and grammar in your document. You can either:

• Let Word check your spelling and grammar as you work, and draw attention to any errors as you make them.

Or

* Check the spelling and grammar in your document when you are ready, and correct any errors at that stage.

Spell/grammar check as you type

When this option is activated, Word identifies incorrect spelling and suspect grammar as you enter and edit your text.

* Words that Word thinks are incorrectly spelt will be underlined with a red, wavy line.

* Words, phrases or sentences that have unusual capitalization or grammatical errors will have a grey wavy line under them.

To fix an error:

1 Right-click on the word.

2 Select an option in the context menu.

* To change the word to one of those listed, click on the correctly spelt word in the list.

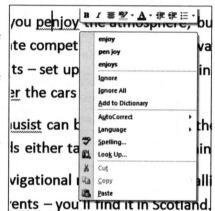

Or

* You can ignore the spelling by choosing **Ignore** or **Ignore All**. If you choose **Ignore**, Word will indicate the word again if it occurs further through the document. If you choose **Ignore All**, Word will not highlight the word again in this working session (it will however highlight the word if it appears in another document or another working session).

Or

* Select **Add to Dictionary** if the spelling is correct and you want to add the word to the dictionary. Once in the dictionary Word will not identify it as an error again.

Grammatical errors can be dealt with in a similar way. When you right-click on the error, Word will display the problem and suggest a remedy if it can. You can choose whether you wish to change your text to that suggested or ignore any suggestion made.

To spell check when you are ready:

1 Display the **Review** tab.

2 Click **Spelling & Grammar** in the **Proofing** group.

• Word will scan your document and prompt you each time a spelling or grammatical error is found.

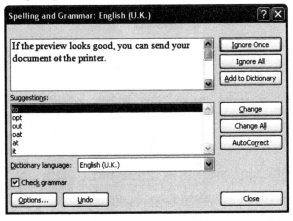

3 Respond to suggestions in the **Spelling and Grammar** dialog box as you see fit.

4 When all errors have been dealt with, a prompt will appear saying that the checking process is complete. Click **OK** to return to your document.

Spelling and grammar options

You can customize the way in which the spelling and grammar feature works.

1 Display the Microsoft Office Menu and click **Word Options**.

2 Select **Proofing** in the categories on the left.

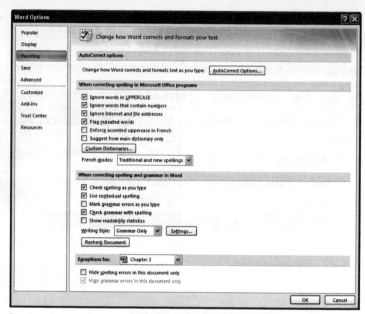

3 Set the options required.

4 Click **OK**.

Spelling and grammar checker not working?

You will know that the spelling or grammar has been turned off or the *Do not check* option has been activated if you find that:

◆ You have opted to have your spelling and/or grammar checked as you type and Word is not highlighting your errors.

Or

◆ You have asked Word to spellcheck your document and it misses your errors and displays this prompt.

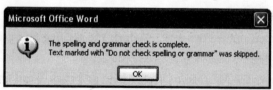

To switch checking on and off:

1 Display the **Review** tab.

2 Click **Set Language** in the **Proofing** tools.

3 Select or clear the **Do not check spelling or grammar** checkbox.

4 Click **Default...** then click **Yes** at the prompt.

5 Click **OK** at the **Language** dialog box.

2.6 Selection techniques

Selection techniques are very important in Word. You need to use them if you want to:

• Copy or move text within a document, or from one document to another.

• Change the formatting of existing text.

• Quickly delete large chunks of text.

There are several ways of selecting text in Word – try some out and use whatever seems easiest to you.

Using the mouse

Click and Drag

1 Move the pointer to one end of the block of text.

2 Click and hold down the left button.

3 Drag over the block of text until you reach its other end.

4 Release the button.

This method tends to work very well for smaller chunks of text – where all the text you want to select is visible on the screen.

If you need to select a big chunk of text, click and drag can be difficult to control – once your text starts to scroll, things move very quickly and it can be hard to see what is being selected.

Click – [Shift] – Click

This method is often easier to control than Click and Drag.

1 Click at one end of the text to position the insertion point.

2 Move the mouse pointer (do not hold down the button) to the other end of the text.

3 Hold down [Shift] and click the left button.

All the text between the insertion point and the mouse pointer should be selected. If it isn't, you most probably released [Shift] *before* you clicked – try again if this is the case!

Both the Click and Drag and the Click – [Shift] – Click methods can be used to select any amount of text.

Standard units of text

If you are selecting a standard unit of text – a word, a sentence, a paragraph or the whole document – there are some special selection techniques that you might like to try instead of those described above.

To select:

♦ A *word* – double-click on it.

♦ A *sentence* – hold down [Ctrl] and click anywhere within it.

♦ A *paragraph* – double-click in the selection bar to the left of the paragraph *or* triple-click anywhere within it.

♦ *The whole document* – triple-click in the selection bar.

To deselect any unit of text:

♦ Click anywhere in your text, or press one of the arrow keys.

Using the keyboard

If you prefer working with the keyboard rather than the mouse, there are several techniques you can try. Selecting text using the keyboard is really a variation on moving through your document using it (see section 2.3). Try these selection methods. All work from the insertion point.

To select a character or line at a time:

* Hold down [Shift] and press the right, left, up or down arrow (cursor) keys until you have selected the text required.

To select right or left, a word at a time:

* Hold down both [Shift] and [Ctrl] and press the right or left arrow key until you have selected the text you need.

To select up or down a paragraph at a time:

* Hold down both [Shift] and [Ctrl] and press the up or down arrow key until you have selected the required text.

Other useful ones are:

* [Shift]-[End] to select to the end of the line.
* [Shift]-[Home] to select to the start of the line.
* [Shift]-[Ctrl]-[Home] to select to the start of the document.
* [Shift]-[Ctrl]-[End] to select to the end of the document.
* [Ctrl]-[A] to select the whole document.

Experiment with the various options as you work.

2.7 Cut, Copy and Paste

When working on a document, you will sometimes find that you have entered the correct text but it's in the wrong place! It may be that it should be somewhere else in that document, or you might want it to go into another document. You could delete the text and type it in again at the correct place, but it's much quicker (especially if it's more than a couple of words) to move or copy the text to its new location.

- You can *move* the text from its current position and place it elsewhere in the same or another document.

- If you want to keep the text, but repeat it in another place in the same or another document, you can *copy* it.

You can move or copy any amount of text – a word, several sentences or paragraphs, or a whole document – but first you must select it (see section 2.6).

Moving text (cut and paste)

Cut

1 Select the text you want to move.

2 Click the **Cut** button in the **Clipboard** group on the Home tab.

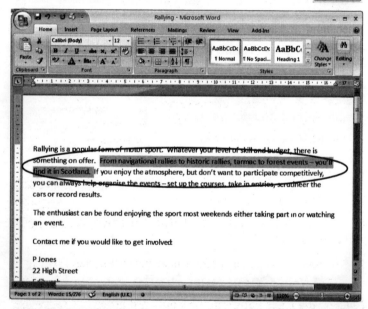

3 Position the insertion point where you want the text to go.

4 Click the **Paste** button in the **Clipboard** group.

The text will appear at the insertion point.

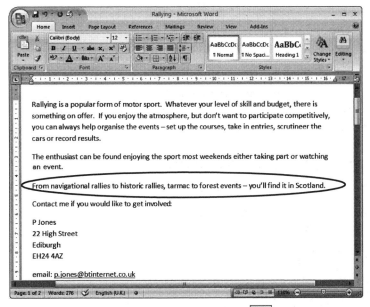

- To specify the format of the pasted item, click the **Paste options** smart tag (it appears below the item) and select the option required.

- ⦿ **K**eep Source Formatting
- ○ Match **D**estination Formatting
- ○ Keep **T**ext Only
- * **S**et Default Paste...

Copying text (copy and paste)

Copy

1 Select the text you want to move.

2 Click the **Copy** button in the **Clipboard** group on the **Home** tab.

3 Position the insertion point where you want the text to go.

4 Click the **Paste** button in the **Clipboard** group.

Office Clipboard

When you cut or copy text (or any object) it is placed in the Office Clipboard. The Clipboard can store up to 24 separate items.

To view the contents of the Clipboard:

* Click the dialog box launcher in the **Clipboard** group.

You can paste the items from the Clipboard into a document in any order.

To paste an individual item:

* Click the item that you want to paste.

To paste all items into your file:

* Click **Paste All** – the items are pasted into your file in the order that you cut or copied them to the Clipboard.

To remove all items from the Clipboard:

* Click **Clear All**.

To delete an item from the Clipboard:

1 Move the pointer over the item – do not click on it or you will paste the item into your file.

2 Click the drop-down arrow at the right.

3 Click **Delete**.

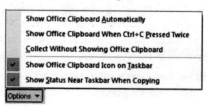

Clipboard options

You can specify how you prefer the Office Clipboard panel to work. At the bottom of the pane, click the **Options** button and select or deselect the options as required.

If you turn on **Show Office Clipboard Icon on Taskbar**, the icon appears towards the right-hand end. If you also select **Show Status Near Taskbar When Copying**, a prompt appears when you copy an item to update you on the status of the Clipboard.

Cut or Copy to a different document

It's usually easier to move or copy text from one document to another if both are open before you start. The document you cut or copy from is called the source document, the one you paste to is the destination.

To move from one open document to another, click on its button on the Taskbar or select the document from the list displayed when you click the Word button on the Taskbar.

To move or copy text from one document to another:

1 Select the text to move or copy in the source document.

2 Click **Cut** or **Copy** in the **Clipboard** group.

3 Display the destination document.

4 Place the insertion point where you want the text to appear.

5 Click **Paste** in the **Clipboard** group.

The text will appear at the insertion point.

Drag and Drop

As an alternative to using Cut or Copy and Paste to move and copy text, you may find Drag and Drop useful. It is especially useful when moving or copying a small amount of text a short distance – i.e. to somewhere else on the screen. If you try to drag and drop text a long way, you will probably find that the text scrolls very quickly on the screen and is hard to control.

To move:

1 Select the text that you want to move.

2 Position the pointer anywhere over the selected text.

3 Click and hold down the left button (notice the ghost insertion point that appears within the selected text area).

4 Drag your mouse until the ghost insertion point is where you want your text moved to.

5 Release the mouse button.

To copy:

♦ Do the same as for moving, but hold down [Ctrl] while you drag.

2.8 Undo, Redo and Repeat

If you make a mistake when you are working, don't panic! You may be able to undo the error by clicking the Undo button on the Quick Access toolbar.

To undo the last thing that you did, e.g. delete text:

♦ Click **Undo** on the Quick Access toolbar.

Or

♦ Use the keyboard shortcut [Ctrl]-[Z].

If you want to undo back to an earlier point, click the drop-down arrow to the right of the Undo tool to display a list of the actions that you can undo. Scroll down the list to find the earliest action you want to undo back to – and click on it. All actions above the one you click will also be undone.

If you change your mind, click the **Redo** tool to put things back as they were.

If the Redo tool is dimmed, you have not undone anything that can be redone!

♦ The **Redo** tool toggles between **Redo**  and **Repeat** depending on the action you have taken.

2.9 Find and Replace

Find

The Find command allows you to locate specific text quickly.

To find specific text:

1 Display the **Home** tab.

2 Click the **Find** button in the **Editing** group.

Or

◆ Press **[Ctrl]-[F]**.

3 Enter the text that you are looking for in the **Find what:** field on the **Find** tab.

4 Click **Find Next** until you locate the text required.

5 Close the dialog box.

To highlight all occurrences of the text in your document:

1 Display the **Find** tab in the **Find and Replace** dialog box – press **[Ctrl]-[F]**.

2 Click **Reading Highlight** then click **Highlight All**.

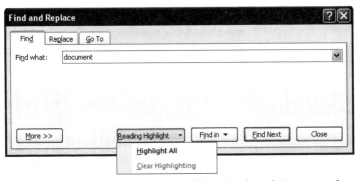

The number of matching items will be displayed. You can then either click on your document and scroll through it to see what has been highlighted, or, if you prefer, close the Find and Replace dialog box and then scroll through your document.

To remove the highlighting:

1 Return to the **Find and Replace** dialog box if necessary.

2 Click **Reading Highlight** and then **Clear Highlighting**.

To specify find options:

1 Click **More...** on the **Find** tab.

2 Select the options as required (see below).

3 Click **Find Next** until you locate the text that you seek.

4 Close the dialog box.

Search options

Search   Choose *All*, or specify the direction you want to search in from the insertion point – *Up* or *Down*.

Match case   Use the capitalization specified in the Find/Replace fields.

Find whole words only   Don't locate the text string embedded within a word, e.g. if you search for 'bed', and select this option, it will ignore the 'bed' in 'embedded'.

Use wildcards   Lets you use '?' to mean any letter, or '*' for any string of characters. Entering 'th?n' would find 'then', 'than', 'thin', etc. 'P*er' would find 'Peter', 'publisher', 'power', etc.

Sounds like   Finds words that sound the same, even if spelt differently, e.g. 'bare' would find 'bare' and 'bear'.

Find all word forms   Useful if you have singular and plural versions of a word to replace, e.g. 'dog' with 'cat' and also 'dogs' with 'cats'. Or different tenses of a verb, e.g. 'run' to 'walk' and 'ran' to 'walked'. Or different adjective forms, e.g. 'better' to 'worse' and 'best' to 'worst'. The use of **Replace All** is not recommended with this option! If you use **Find Next,** you will be given replace options.

Format   Specify the formatting in the various dialog boxes.

Special   Used to locate special characters, e.g. non-breaking spaces, paragraph marks, etc.

No formatting If you have specified formatting you can cancel it quickly using this option.

The other options are: **Match prefix, Match suffix, Ignore punctuation characters** and **Ignore white-space characters.**

Replace

Replace can be a very useful tool – especially if you've spelt a name wrong throughout a document!!

1 Display the **Home** tab.

2 Click the **Replace** button in the **Editing** group.

Or

• Press **[Ctrl]-[F]** and select the **Replace** tab in the dialog box.

3 Enter the text you want to find in the **Find what:** field.

4 Specify any options and formatting as necessary.

5 Enter the replacement text in the **Replace with:** field.

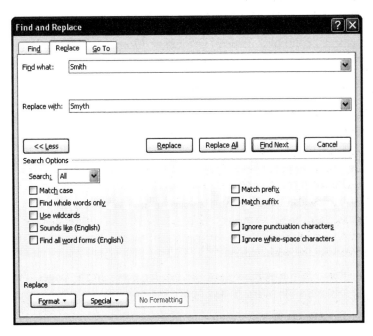

6 Specify any options and formatting as necessary.

7 Click **Find Next**.

8 Word will highlight the first occurrence of the text it finds.

9 Click **Replace** to replace this one occurrence (Word will then move onto the next), or click **Find Next** to ignore it and move onto the next one.

Or

10 Click **Replace All** to replace all occurrences automatically (be careful with this one!).

2.10 Views

The way your document appears on your screen is called a 'view'. There are several views to choose from. The one that you are likely to use most often is Print Layout, and perhaps Draft view.

Print Layout

The view most commonly used is Print Layout view. In this view margins, columns, pictures, headers and footers, etc. are all displayed. The document is displayed as it would if printed.

In Print Layout view the top and bottom margin areas are displayed. These areas may contain headers and footers, or they could be empty. You can opt to show or hide the white space in the top and bottom margin areas on your screen.

To hide the white space:

1 Position the pointer over the top or bottom edge of a page – it becomes the **Hide White Space** ⊞ pointer.

2 Double-click.

To show the white space:

1 Position the pointer over the border between the pages – it becomes the **Show White Space** ⬍ pointer.

2 Double-click.

Full Screen Reading layout

This view is useful when reading a document. The Ribbon and scroll bars are cleared off the screen and the document is enlarged to make it easier to read it.

• You can cancel this view by pressing [Esc].

Web Layout

This view displays your page as it would appear in a Web browser. This view is used automatically when you are preparing a blog entry (see Chapter 13).

Outline view

Outline view is used to display the structure of your document. We will discuss it in greater detail in Chapter 7.

Draft view

In Draft view, the text of the document is displayed without the margins, columns, pictures, etc. that you would get in Print Layout. It is useful if you want to concentrate on your document without the distraction of page layout and graphics.

You can change from one view to another at any time.

To change views:

• Click a View button on the Status bar.

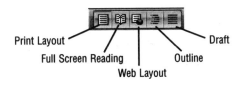

Or

• Click a View button in the **Document Views** group on the View tab.

2.11   Compare side by side

If you have two documents open, you can view them at the same time by using the Compare Side by Side view. This is useful when you want to compare the contents of two documents, or move or copy text from one to another.

To view two open documents side by side:

1   Open both documents.

2   Select the **View** tab on the Ribbon.

3   In the **Window** group, click **View Side by Side**.

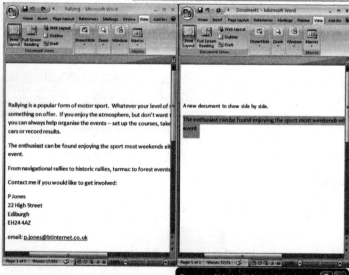

If you have more than two documents open, the **Compare Side by Side** dialog box will appear. It lists all open documents so that you can choose the one you wish to compare with – select it and click **OK**.

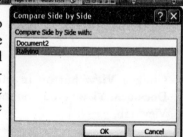

You can then cut/copy and paste, or drag and drop from one of the displayed documents to the other.

To close Side by Side viewing:

• Click the **Window** button and click **View Side by Side** again.

Synchronous Scrolling

The Synchronous Scrolling option allows you to scroll both windows simultaneously. It is turned on automatically when you choose to View Side by Side. You can switch the option on and off by clicking Synchronous Scrolling in the Window group.

2.12 Insert symbols

Most of the characters that you will use – alpha, numeric and punctuation – are to be found on the standard keyboard. There are however a considerable number of other characters that you might want to use in your document, e.g. copyright or trademark symbols, or picture characters like envelopes, smiley faces or scissors. These can be created either using the keyboard, or from the **Insert Symbol** dialog box.

Symbols that you can insert using the keyboard include:

Symbol		You type
©	Copyright	(c)
®	Registered	(r)
™	Trade mark	(tm)
•	Euro	[Alt]-[Ctrl]-[E]
☺	Smiley face	:) or :-)
☹	Sad face	:(or :-(
☺	Face	:l or :-l
½	Half	1/2
¼	Quarter	1/4
¾	Three-quarters	3/4

If you type the keyboard shortcuts for these, the symbol appears automatically. If you don't want the symbol – you want what you actually typed – press [Ctrl]-[Z] or click **Undo**. The symbol will change back to the typed characters.

To access the full range of symbols:

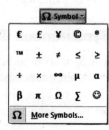

1 Click the **Symbol** button in the **Symbols** group on the **Insert** tab.

2 Select the symbol from those displayed.

Or

• Click **More Symbols…** to open the **Symbol** dialog box.

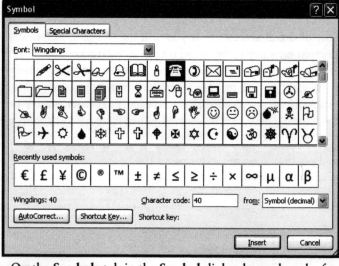

3 On the **Symbols** tab in the **Symbol** dialog box select the font that contains the symbol you want.

• Initially you will just have to explore the fonts to see what is there, but the standard picture fonts are Webdings and Wingdings, Wingdings 2 and Wingdings 3.

4 Scroll through the characters and select the one you want.

5 Click **Insert**.

6 Close the **Symbol** dialog box.

2.13 Print Preview

The final step with a document is often printing it. But before sending a document to print, it's a good idea to preview it.

The preview will display a full page of your document on the screen at once (more than one page if you wish) so that you can check how the finished page will look. Preview is useful if you want to check the balance of text/white space/graphics on a page.

* How much space does your text take up?

* Is the balance of 'white space' (blank areas) and text okay?

If the preview looks good, you can send your document to the printer. If not, you might want to edit the layout to try to get a better-looking document.

To preview a document:

1 Click the Microsoft Office button.

2 Click the arrow beside **Print** and choose **Print Preview**.

- A full-page preview of your document will appear on the screen.

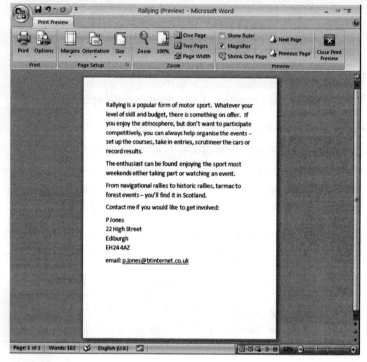

Zoom

If you move the pointer over a page in Print Preview, it looks like a magnifying glass with a + (plus sign) on it.

- Click the left button to zoom in on your document so that you can read it more clearly.

When you are zoomed in, the magnifying glass pointer has a – (minus sign) on it.

- Click to zoom out to get an overview of the page again.

Editing text in Print Preview

If you zoom in on your text, and notice something that you want to change, you can edit your document. To edit in Print Preview you must switch the magnifier off.

To edit a document in Print Preview:

1 Deselect the **Magnifier** checkbox in the **Preview** group on the Print Preview Ribbon.

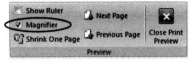

2 Edit your document as necessary.

3 To activate the magnifier again, tick the **Magnifier** checkbox.

Print Preview Ribbon

The buttons on the Ribbon can be used to control the display of your document in Print Preview, specify document layout preferences and set print options.

Print group

• **Print** displays the **Print** dialog box where you can specify what pages to print and set the number of copies required.

• **Options** displays the **Options** dialog box where you can set those print options that control how the document looks on the screen and when it is printed.

Page Setup

The buttons in this group allow you to change the margins (the distance between the text and the edge of the paper), the orientation (either landscape or portrait) and the paper size.

You can also launch the Page Setup dialog box to access all the page setup options available.

Zoom

• This group gives options that allow you to control the zoom level and the number of pages displayed at one time.

Preview

* **Show Ruler** toggles the display of the vertical and horizontal rulers.

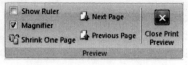

* **Magnifier** (see previous page).

* **Shrink One Page** reduces the document size by one page, and can be very useful in situations where the last page in the document contains just two or three lines. Word will decrease the size of each font used in the document to get the text to fit on to one page less.

* **Next Page** and **Previous Page** move through the pages in your document. There are also buttons at the bottom of the vertical scrollbar that move you to the next or previous page.

* **Close Print Preview** exits Print Preview and returns you to your document.

2.14   Print

To print one copy of your whole document:

1 Display the Microsoft Office button menu.

2 Click the arrow to the right of **Print**.

3 Select **Quick Print**.

To specify print options before you print:

1 Display the Microsoft Office button menu.

2 Click **Print**.

Or

* Click the arrow to the right of **Print** and select **Print**.

3 Complete the dialog box as required.

4 Click **OK**.

Summary

In this chapter we have discussed the basic skills required to create a new document, enter and edit text and print your file. We have looked at:

* File handling, e.g. creating, saving, closing and opening documents

* Entering and editing text

* Moving around your document

* Spell and grammar checking

* Selection techniques using the mouse and the keyboard

* Moving and copying text

* The Office Clipboard

* Undo, Redo and Repeat

* Find and Replace

* Document views and Compare Side by Side

* Inserting symbols

* Print Preview and Print.

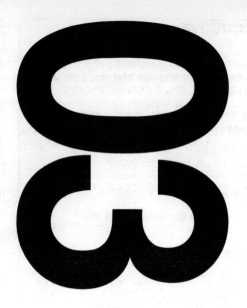

03

formatting

In this chapter you will learn:

- how to apply font formatting
- some paragraph formatting options
- how to apply borders and shading
- about tabs and indents

3.1 Font formatting

One way of enhancing your text is to apply font formatting to it. The effects can be applied to individual characters in your document. You can underline them, increase their size, change their colour, or make them bold or italic.

Unless you specify otherwise, characters are formatted in the Calibri font with a size of 11 point. (There are 72 points to an inch – this text, for example, is set to 10 point.)

The most commonly used font formatting options are found in the Font group on the Home tab.

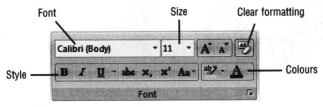

To format text, either:

• Set the format as you enter text.

Or

• Enter your text and then apply the formatting to it.

To format text as you key it in:

1 Select the formatting option.

2 Enter your text.

3 Switch the option off when you reach the end of the text (or select a different formatting option).

To format existing text:

1 Select the text.

2 Choose the formatting option required.

3 Deselect your text.

3.2 Font styles

The **bold**, *italic*, <u>single underline</u>, ~~strikethrough~~, subscript and superscript formatting options are toggles – you switch them on and off in the same way. It is easiest to set them using the buttons in the Font group. Click the button to turn the option on or off.

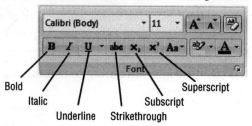

Bold
Italic
Underline
Strikethrough
Subscript
Superscript

Keyboard shortcuts

You can switch these formats on and off with the shortcuts:

[Ctrl]-[B]	Bold	[Ctrl]-[I]	Italic
[Ctrl]-[U]	Underline	[Ctrl]-[=]	Subscript
[Ctrl]-[Shift]-[+]	Superscript		

Underline options

The default underline format is a single line. You can choose an alternative from the drop-down list that is displayed when you click the arrow to the right of the Underline button.

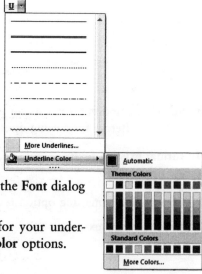

If you cannot find a style that you want in the list, click **More Underlines...** and explore the options in the **Font** dialog box.

You can choose a colour for your underline from the **Underline Color** options.

3.3 Change Case

There may be times when you manage to type in the right text, but the capitalization on it is wrong. It may be that you have left the Caps Lock on in error and you have ended up with your upper and lower case characters transposed. There is no need to re-type when this problem occurs – you simply change case to fix (or at least improve) the situation.

To change case:

1 Select the text you want to format.

2 Click the **Change Case** button.

3 Choose an option from the list.

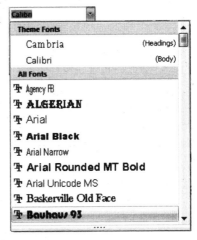

It may be that by changing case, you do not get the capitalization exactly as you want it. Pick the option that gets you closest, then edit from there if necessary. It will nearly always be quicker than retyping!

3.4 Font, size and colour

To change the font:

1 Click the arrow to the right of the **Font** button.

2 Scroll through the list until you see the font you want to use.

3 Click on it.

To change the font size:

1 Click the arrow to the right of the **Font Size** button.

2 Scroll through the list of sizes until you see the one you want to use.

3 Click on it.

Grow Font/Shrink Font

You can also use the **Grow Font** and **Shrink Font** buttons to change the font size.

Each time you click the Grow Font button, the size increases to the next in the font size list. When you click the Shrink Font button, it decreases the font size to the next on the list.

Keyboard shortcuts

[Ctrl]-[Shift]-[>]   Grow Font

[Ctrl]-[Shift]-[<]   Shrink Font

To change the font colour:

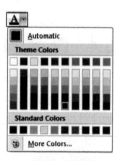

1 Click the drop-down arrow to the right of the Font Color command button.

2 Select the colour you want to use.

Live Preview

If Live Preview is enabled, selected text adopts the font formatting option that the mouse pointer is over. This allows you to see its affect before you choose it.

You can switch Live Preview on and off in Word Options.

1 Click the Microsoft Office button and then Word Options.

2 Select the Popular category on the left.

3 Select or deselect the Enable Live Preview checkbox.

4 Click OK.

3.5   Highlight text

To highlight your text (the equivalent to using a marker pen on it) use the Highlight button in the Font group. The highlight prints out – if you have a black and white printer, the colour will appear as grey shading behind your text.

To apply highlight to existing text:

1   Select the text to be highlighted.

2   Click the **Text Highlight Color** button to use the default yellow highlight.

No Color

Stop Highlighting

Or

3   Click the drop-down arrow to the right of the button, then select a colour.

Or

4   Choose a colour from the **Text Highlight Color** options (without first selecting text).

5   Click and drag over the text (the mouse pointer looks like the I-beam with a marker pen attached).

6   Click the **Highlight** button again to switch the feature off (or choose **Stop Highlighting** from the drop-down options).

To remove highlight from existing text:

1   Select the text that has the highlight applied to it.

2   Display the Highlight options and select **No Color**.

Automatic word selection

To format a word, position the insertion point anywhere inside it, and then apply the formatting. By default Word automatically formats the whole word surrounding the insertion point. Automatic word selection is controlled in Word Options:

1   Click the Microsoft Office button and choose **Word Options**.

2   Select the **Advanced** category.

3   Set the **When selecting, automatically select entire word** option as required.

3.6 And yet more options...

Other formatting options can be found in the Font dialog box.
Try some out on your text.

1 Click the **Font** dialog box launcher at the bottom right of the
Font group.

2 Select a tab – **Font** or **Character Spacing**.

3 Choose the effects you want. A preview of your selection is
displayed in the Preview window.

4 Click **OK** to apply the effects, or **Cancel** to return to your
document without making any changes.

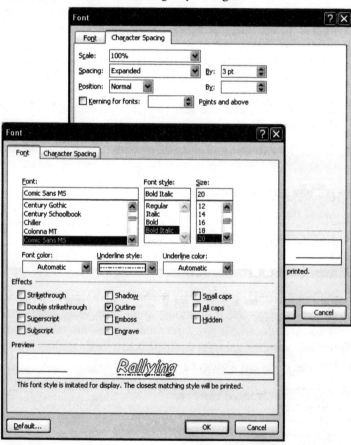

3.7 Default font

The default font is the one that is used every time you create a new document – initially it is set to the Calibri font with a size of 11 points. If you or your company prefer to use a different font for most of your documents, you can change the default.

To change the default font:

1 Click the **Font** dialog box launcher at the bottom right of the Font group.

2 Select the font, font size, etc. that you want to use in the **Font** dialog box.

3 Click **Default...**

4 At the prompt, click:

* **Yes** if you want the change to affect all new documents based on the Normal template.

* **No** if you just want to affect the current document.

* **Cancel** if you have changed you mind.

5 Click **OK** at the **Font** dialog box.

3.8 Clear formatting

If you want to clear all the font formatting from some text, the quickest option is often the Clear formatting command.

To clear formatting:

1 Select the text whose formatting you wish to clear.

2 Click the **Clear Formatting** button on the **Font** group.

Or

* Use the keyboard shortcut [**Ctrl**]-[**Spacebar**].

All the formatting will be removed from the selection, leaving just plain text.

3.9 Paragraph formatting

Some formatting options are applied to complete paragraphs, regardless of whether the paragraph consists of a few words or several lines. A paragraph is created in Word each time you press [Enter]. The heading at the top of this page is a paragraph and this text is a paragraph. Each time you press [Enter] you insert a paragraph mark into the document.

The most commonly used paragraph formatting options are found in the Paragraph group on the Home tab.

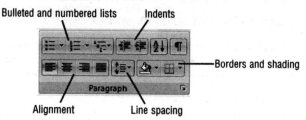

Bulleted and numbered lists   Indents

Borders and shading

Paragraph

Alignment   Line spacing

The default paragraph formatting options (those normally used) give you a left aligned paragraph, with 1.15 line spacing with a 10 pt space after each paragraph. If this is not the formatting you require you can change it.

Show/hide formatting marks

You can toggle the display of the paragraph marks and other non-printing characters in your document using the Show/Hide ¶ button in the Paragraph group. These do not print out even if they are displayed on your screen.

Other non-printing characters, e.g. a dot for each space or an arrow for each [Tab] keypress, are also displayed when you opt to Show the formatting marks. By default, no marks are displayed when the option is set to Hide. You can opt to show some marks even when the Hide status is operational, using the Word Options dialog box.

1 Click the Microsoft Office button, then Word Options.

2 Select the Display category.

3 Select the marks that you always want to display.

4 Click OK.

Specifying paragraph formatting

When applying paragraph formatting to text you can either:

* Set the paragraph format, then enter your text.

Or

* Enter your text and apply the paragraph formatting later.

To change the formatting of consecutive paragraphs, select them first, and then change the formatting.

Automatic paragraph selection

To apply a format to an existing paragraph, position the insertion point anywhere inside it, then apply the formatting.

To format paragraphs as you enter text:

1 Select the formatting options – alignment, line spacing, etc.

2 Type in your text. Each time you press [Enter], the format-ting options will carry forward to the next paragraph.

3 Press [**Enter**] at the end of the last paragraph that you want the formatting applied to.

4 Select the next formatting option(s).

To format existing paragraphs:

1 Select the paragraph(s) that you want to format.

2 Specify the formatting.

3.10   Alignment

Paragraphs can be aligned to the left, right or centre, or justified (see the examples overleaf). The default is left, where the text is flush with the left margin and has a ragged right-hand edge.

To set alignment:

* Click the appropriate button in the **Paragraph** group.

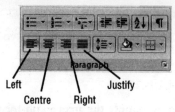

Left   Justify
      Centre Right

Keyboard shortcuts

[Ctrl]-[L] Align left   [Ctrl]-[E] Centre align

[Ctrl]-[R] Align right   [Ctrl]-[J] Justify

| Justify |

Rallying is a popular form of motor sport. Whatever your level of skill and budget there is something on offer. If you enjoy the atmosphere, but don't want to participate competitively, you can always help organise the events – set up the courses, take in entries, scrutineer the cars or record results.

| Right align |

The enthusiast can be found enjoying the sport most weekends either taking part

| Left align | *or watching an event.*

From navigational rallies to historic rallies, tarmac to forest events – you'll find it in Scotland.

| Centre |

Contact me if you would like to get involved:

P Jones
22 High Street
Edinburgh
EH24 4AZ
Email: p.jones@btinternet.co.uk

3.11 Line spacing

Initially, your line spacing is set to 1.15. You can set different spacing using the Line Spacing tool.

1 Select the text you wish to change.

2 Click the drop-down arrow beside the **Line Spacing** tool.

3 Select a **Line Spacing** option.

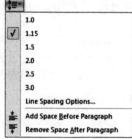

To set line spacing other than those listed, click **Line Spacing Options...** and specify the value in the **Line Spacing** field in the **Format Paragraph** dialog box.

Line spacing options

1	Single line spacing. Accommodates the largest font size in the line, and adds about 10% extra space.
1.5	One and a half that of single.
2.0	Double that of single.
Multiple	Specifies the spacing as a set number of lines, e.g. 1.15 sets each line 1.15 line depths apart. The number is specified in the **At:** field.
Exactly	Fixed line spacing, measured in points. Set the value in the **At:** field.
At Least	Sets minimum size, which Word will adjust as needed to accommodate larger font sizes and graphics. Set the value, in points, in the **At:** field.

Keyboard shortcuts

[Ctrl]-[1]	Single line spacing
[Ctrl]-[5]	1.5 line spacing
[Ctrl]-[2]	Double line spacing

The default spacing before a paragraph is 12 point and after is 10 point. Either or both spaces can be present.

To **add or remove default spacing:**

1 Select the text you wish to change.

2 Click the arrow beside the **Line Spacing** tool and click **Add/Remove Space Before Paragraph** or **Add/Remove Space After Paragraph**.

The selected paragraph must currently have a space after, but not before.

You can control the exact amount of spacing that appears before and after a paragraph in the Format paragraph dialog box.

To specify the spacing before or after a paragraph:

1 Display the **Paragraph** dialog box (click the dialog box launcher, or click **Line Spacing Options…** in the Line Spacing drop-down list).

2 Set the **Spacing Before** and/or **Spacing After** fields as required.

3 Click **OK**.

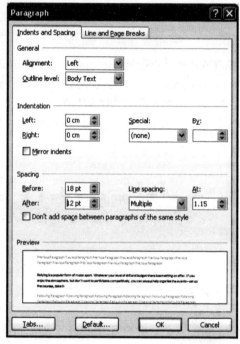

Or

4 Display the **Page Layout** tab.

5 Set the **Before** and **After** options in the **Spacing** fields in the **Paragraph** group.

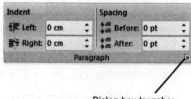

Dialog box launcher

3.12 Borders and shading

Borders and shading can emphasize areas. They can be applied to whole paragraphs or selected text within a paragraph.

To place a border:

1 Select the text or paragraph(s).

2 Click the arrow by the **Borders** button to display the **Borders** options.

3 Select a border from the list.

To remove a border:

1 Select the text or paragraph(s) you want to remove borders from.

2 Display the **Borders** drop-down list.

3 Click the **No Border** option.

To customize your borders:

1 Choose **Borders and Shading...** from the **Borders** list.

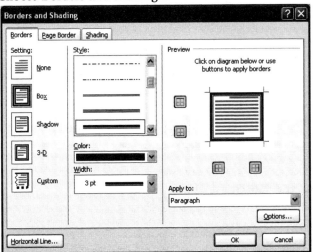

2 On the **Borders** tab, select a **Setting**, e.g. Box, Shadow, 3D.

3 Choose the **Style, Color** and/or **Width** (measured in points).

4 Click **OK**.

To switch individual borders on and off, click the border tools or the lines around the example in the Preview window.

If you choose Custom border from the Setting list, you can specify different borders for different sides of the selected area.

To set custom borders:

1 Choose **Custom** in the **Setting** options.

2 Choose the **Style**, **Color** and/or **Width**.

3 Click the appropriate button or line in the Preview panel.

4 Repeat steps 2–3 to specify all the borders then click **OK**.

Horizontal line

Horizontal lines can be used in any document, and are very effective on Web pages.

To add a horizontal line:

1 Position the insertion point where you want the line to be.

2 Display the **Borders** list.

3 Click **Horizontal Line**.

To choose a custom horizontal line style:

1 Place the insertion point where you want the line.

2 Display the **Borders and Shading** dialog box.

3 Click **Horizontal Line...** on the **Borders** tab.

4 At the **Horizontal Line** dialog box, choose a line style.

5 Click **OK**.

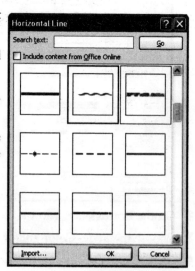

Shading

You can use the Shading button in the Paragraph group to add shading to your text or paragraph(s).

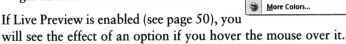

1 Select the text or paragraph(s) you wish to add shading to.

2 Click the **Shading** tool in the **Paragraph** group.

3 Pick a colour, or click **More Colors...** to get additional colours and shades.

If Live Preview is enabled (see page 50), you will see the effect of an option if you hover the mouse over it.

To remove shading from your text or paragraph(s):

1 Select the text or paragraph(s) to remove shading from.

2 Click the **Shading** tool in the **Paragraph** group.

3 Choose **No Color**.

There are further options in the Borders and Shading dialog box.

1 Select the text or paragraph(s) you wish to add shading to.

2 Display the **Borders and Shading** dialog box.

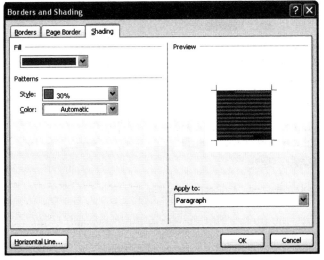

3 On the **Shading** tab choose a **Fill** colour.

4 Select a **Pattern** from the **Style** list.

5 Choose a colour for your pattern from the **Color** list.

6 Click **OK**.

RALLYING

Rallying is a popular form of motor sport. Whatever your level of skill and budget there is something on offer. If you enjoy the atmosphere, but don't want to participate competitively, you can always help organise the events – set up the courses, take in entries, scrutineer the cars or record results.

The enthusiast can be found enjoying the sport most weekends either taking part or watching an event.

From navigational rallies to historic rallies, tarmac to forest events – <u>you'll find it in Scotland</u>.

Contact me if you would like to get involved:

P Jones
22 High Street
Edinburgh
EH24 4AZ

Email: <u>p.jones@btinternet.co.uk</u>

Black and white

The higher the percentage of the grey fill, the harder it gets to read your text (unless you change the font colour). If you choose black, Word automatically displays the text as white.

3.13 Lists

Bulleted lists

To add bullets as you enter your text:

1 Click the **Bullets** button ≔ in the **Paragraph** group.

2 Type in the text for the first bullet point.

3 Press **[Enter]** to create a new paragraph – it is automatically given a bullet.

4 After all the bullet points have been typed, press **[Enter]** twice, without entering any text, and the bullets are switched off.

To add or remove bullets from existing paragraphs:

1 Select the paragraphs.

2 Click the **Bullets** button to toggle them on or off.

To change the bullet style:

1 Select the paragraphs.

2 Click the arrow beside the **Bullets** button to display a list of options.

3 Select the bullet from the **Recently Used Bullets** or the **Bullet Library**.

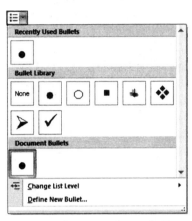

To define a new bullet:

1 Click **Define New Bullet...** at the bottom of the bullet options.

2 At the **Define New Bullet** dialog box, click **Symbol...** to open the **Symbol** dialog box.

3 Select a font, then a character, and click **OK** to return to the **Define New Bullet** dialog box.

4 Click **Font...** to display the **Font** dialog box – specify the size and colour and other font formatting options for your bullet, and click **OK**.

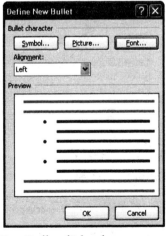

5 Click **OK** to close the **Define New Bullet** dialog box.

- Alternatively, click **Picture...** and choose a bullet from the picture options.

Numbered lists

You can number paragraphs in the same way as you apply bullets – just use the Numbering button in the Paragraph group.

Word keeps your numbering up to date as you edit your list. If you add extra paragraphs into your list, delete some, move or copy them, Word will automatically renumber the list.

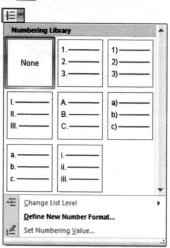

- To set an alternative numbering style, click the arrow to the right of the numbering tool to display the Library and choose a format.

You can also define a new number format if you wish.

To define a new format:

1 Click **Define New Number Format...** in the list.

2 Select a **Number style** from the list.

3 Click the **Font...** button and set the formatting, e.g. bold, size, etc. for the style as required.

4 In the **Number format:** field add any standard characters, e.g. full stop after the number, brackets after or around it.

5 Set the **Alignment**.

6 Click **OK**.

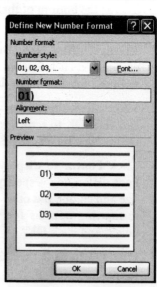

If you are working through a document, switching numbering on and off, a smart tag may appear automatically so that you can specify how you wish your numbering to proceed.

Either ignore the smart tag, or click it to select the **Restart Numbering** option.

You can also control a numbered list from the pop-up menu.

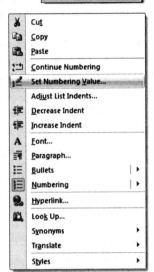

1 Select the list and right-click on it.

2 Choose **Continue Numbering** to carry on from the previous numbered list.

Or

3 Choose **Set Numbering Value...** and specify whether to start a new list, continue numbering or start numbering at a specific value.

3.14 Units of measurement

When you want to specify things like margins, indent positions or tabs, you do so by stating the measurement that you want these markers positioned at. The measurements can be in inches, centimetres, millimetres, points or picas. Most people will probably use centimetres as their preferred unit. You can easily change the unit.

To change the units:

1 Click the Microsoft Office button and then **Word Options**.

2 Select **Advanced** in the category list.

3 Scroll down to the **Display** options.

4 Select the **Unit of measurement** required.

5 Click **OK**.

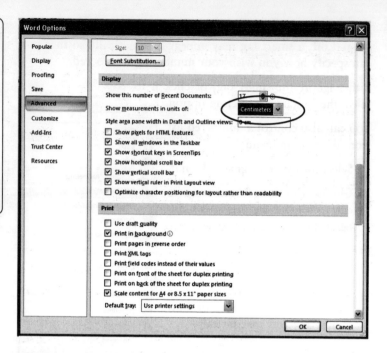

3.15 Indents

Paragraphs normally run from the left to the right margin. As you enter text, it extends along the line until it reaches the right margin and then automatically wraps to the next line, unless you press [Enter].

In fact, your text actually runs from the left indent marker to the right indent marker (not from the left to right margin) – but the indent markers are flush with the margins unless you set them differently.

If you want to leave some white space between your text and the margin you can move the indent markers inwards. Paragraphs that do not have text running from margin to margin are in-dented paragraphs.

You can change the position of the left indent using the buttons in the Paragraph group, or you can change both the left and right indent from the Paragraph dialog box.

To change the left indent using the buttons:

1 Select the paragraphs that you want to indent.

2 Click the **Increase Indent** button ![icon] to move the left indent in to the next tab position (each time you click it the paragraph moves in to the next tab marker).

♦ If you indent too far, click the **Decrease Indent** button ![icon] to move the left edge of the paragraph back out.

To change the indents using the dialog box:

1 Click the launcher to open the **Paragraph** dialog box.

2 Select the **Indents and Spacing** tab.

3 Set the values in the **Left** and **Right** fields in the **Indentation** area – this will be applied to all the lines in your paragraph.

4 Hanging or first line only indent can be set in the **Special** field.

5 Set the amount of hanging or first line indent in the **By** field.

♦ Use the **Preview** to see the effect.

6 Click **OK** to confirm your settings.

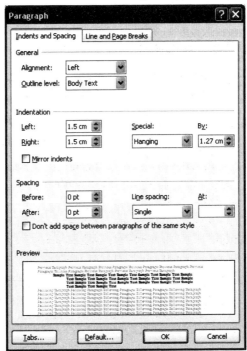

First line indent

> Rallying is a popular form of motor sport. Whatever your level of skill and budget there is something on offer. If you enjoy the atmosphere, but don't want to participate competitively, you can always help organise the events – set up the courses, take in entries, scrutineer the cars or record results.

Indent from left and right

> Rallying is a popular form of motor sport. Whatever your level of skill and budget there is something on offer. If you enjoy the atmosphere, but don't want to participate competitively, you can always help organise the events – set up the courses, take in entries, scrutineer the cars or record results.

Indent from right only

> Rallying is a popular form of motor sport. Whatever your level of skill and budget there is something on offer. If you enjoy the atmosphere, but don't want to participate competitively, you can always help organise the events – set up the courses, take in entries, scrutineer the cars or record results.

Hanging Indent

> Rallying is a popular form of motor sport. Whatever your level of skill and budget there is something on offer. If you enjoy the atmosphere, but don't want to participate competitively, you can always help organise the events – set up the courses, take in entries, scrutineer the cars or record results.

Using the horizontal ruler

If the ruler is displayed, you can use it to set your indents.

To toggle the display of the ruler:

♦ Click the **View Ruler** button at the top of the vertical scroll bar.

The indent markers are the two triangles and the small rectangle below them at the left edge of the text area, and the small triangle at the right edge of it.

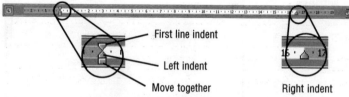

First line indent

Left indent

Move together

Right indent

♦ To set the indent, drag the appropriate marker along the ruler to the correct position.

To improve accuracy when setting indents you can display the exact position of your indent on the ruler as you drag it along.

• Hold [Alt] down while you click and drag.

L ←— 2.54 cm —→ ←— 1.98 cm —→ 14.53 cm

Style button

You can also set the left indents using the Style button to the left of the horizontal ruler.

• Click the button until the indent you require is displayed. Use 🔲 for first line indent or 🔲 for all lines except the first, then click on the lower edge of the ruler to indicate where you want to set your indent.

Make life easy

Don't be tempted to push text along each line using spaces or tabs, or cut lines short by pressing [Enter], to create indented effects. This can result in a lot of extra work and frustration if you need to insert or delete text later.

3.16 Tabs

Tabs are used to align text horizontally, e.g. to align the columns in a list of names and phone numbers. Each time you press [Tab], the insertion point jumps to the next tab position. The default tabs are set every 1.27 cm (½ inch) – the small dark grey marks along the bottom of the ruler indicate their positions – and are left aligned. Tabs can be aligned to the left, right, centre or decimal point, or draw a bar.

Alignment	Effect	Possible usage
Left	Left edge at tab	Any text or numbers
Right	Right edge at tab	Text, or numbers you want to line up on the unit
Centre	Centred under tab	Anything, particularly headings
Decimal	Point under tab	Figures to line up on the decimal point
Bar	Vertical line at tab	To draw a line between columns

If you need to use tabs, and the pre-set ones are not what you require, you must set tabs at the positions you need them.

Using the ruler

To set a tab:

1 Click the Style button to the left of the ruler until you've got the alignment option required.

Left [image] Centre [image] Right [image] Decimal [image] Bar [image]

2 Click on the lower half of the ruler to set the tab.

To move a tab:

◆ Drag it along the ruler to its correct position.

To delete a tab:

◆ Drag it down, off the ruler, and drop it.

Using the dialog box

To display the Tabs dialog box:

1 Open the **Paragraph** dialog box – click the dialog box launcher in the **Paragraph** group.

2 Click **Tabs...**

Or

◆ Double-click on the lower half of the ruler.

To set a tab:

1 Type the **Tab stop position**.

2 Select an **Alignment** option.

3 Choose a **Leader** character (if required).

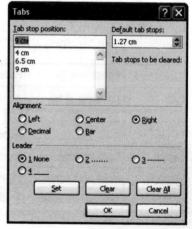

4 Click **Set**.

5 Repeat 1–4 until all tabs have been set.

6 Click **OK**.

To delete a tab:

1 Select the tab in the Tab stop position list.

2 Click **Clear** to remove that tab only.

Or

3 Click **Clear All** to remove all tabs.

4 Click **OK**.

Leader characters

Leader characters are useful to guide the eye along the line when your columns are not close together. When you press [Tab] with a leader character set, the character automatically infills the space between the columns.

Issue 40	**NEWSLETTER**	July 2007

Contents

Letter from the Editor ....Page 1

Progress Report on new branch office...Page 2

Latest fixture results – from the sports club ....Page 4

New Faces...Page 6

Special offers and competitions ....Page 7

ଔଔଔଔଔଔଔଔ

In this example, the issue number is at the left margin, a centre tab is set in the middle for the 'NEWSLETTER' heading, and a right tab is set at the margin for the date. The Contents subheading is aligned with the same centre tab as 'NEWSLETTER'. For the lower part of the page, the centre tab was cleared, and the right tab had a leader character added.

3.17 Format Painter

If you need to apply the same formatting to different pieces of text throughout your document, you could use the Format Painter to 'paint' the formatting onto your text.

1 Select some text with the formatting that you want to use.

2 Click the **Format Painter** button in the **Clipboard** group.

3 Click and drag over the text to paint on the formatting.

If you want to paint the formatting onto several separate pieces of text, double-clicking the Format Painter to lock it. When you have finished, click the button again to unlock it, or press [**Esc**].

Summary

In this chapter we have discussed basic formatting including:

* Font formatting that you can switch on and off, e.g. bold, italic, underline, strikethrough, subscript and superscript

* Font formatting options that you can select from a range, e.g. font, font size, font colour, highlight

* The Grow Font and Shrink Font buttons

* Highlighting text

* Clearing formatting

* Show/Hide formatting symbols

* Paragraph formatting, e.g. alignment, line spacing, borders and shading

* Bulleted and numbered lists

* Increasing and decreasing the indent on paragraphs

* Tabs to control the document layout

* Format Painter.

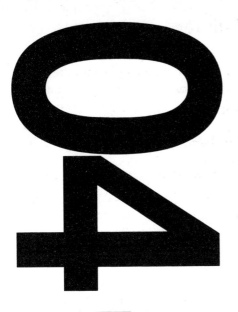

04

page setup

In this chapter you will learn:

- how to create sections
- about margins, orientation and multiple page layouts
- how to use columns
- how to set paper size and source
- about hyphenation
- about borders and colour options
- how to align text vertically

4.1 Sections

Sections are used in every Word document. Up until now, the documents we have looked at have consisted of one section only. If you look at the left of the Status bar, you will see information about the current position of the insertion point within your document. In this case it is in Page 2, Section 1 of a 4-page document.

`Page: 2    Section: 1    Page: 2 of 4`

• If you cannot see this information, right-click on the Status bar and select **Section** from the Customize Status Bar list.

Many documents contain only one section. Others have several. You may need to divide one up into sections for various reasons:

• Part of the document has a different orientation, i.e. some of the pages are landscape, others are portrait.

• Some of the pages may need different margin settings.

• You might want to display a different number of columns on different parts of a page – perhaps for a newsletter layout.

When you change a page layout feature in a dialog box and apply it from **This point forward**, Word automatically inserts a section break for you. You can also insert breaks as needed using the Breaks command.

To insert a section break:

1 Display the **Page Layout** tab.

2 Click **Breaks** in the **Page Setup** group.

3 Choose the type of **Section Break** required.

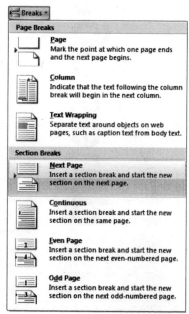

Breaks

Page Breaks

Page
Mark the point at which one page ends and the next page begins.

Column
Indicate that the text following the column break will begin in the next column.

Text Wrapping
Separate text around objects on web pages, such as caption text from body text.

Section Breaks

Next Page
Insert a section break and start the new section on the next page.

Continuous
Insert a section break and start the new section on the same page.

Even Page
Insert a section break and start the new section on the next even-numbered page.

Odd Page
Insert a section break and start the new section on the next odd-numbered page.

Section break options

◆ **Next Page** inserts a section break at the insertion point and starts the next section at the top of the next page.

◆ **Continuous** inserts a section break at the insertion point, and starts the next section immediately.

◆ **Even Page** inserts a section break and starts the next section on the next even numbered page.

◆ **Odd Page** inserts a section break and starts the next section on the next odd numbered page.

Section breaks are always displayed in Draft view. You can also display them in Print Layout view if you show your non-printing characters (see page 54).

::Section Break (Next Page)::

Once you have inserted a section break, you can format each section individually. To find out which section your insertion point is in, check the Section indicator on the Status bar.

To remove a section break:

1 Select the section break (show the non-printing characters if necessary).

2 Press [Delete].

When you remove a section break, the section that was above it adopts the formatting of the one that was below. A section break controls the formatting of the section that precedes it.

To change the formatting of a section:

1 Place the insertion point within the section.

2 Change the layout of the section as required.

Section formatting options include:

Margins, orientation, columns, paper size, paper source (for a printer), page borders, vertical alignment of text and line numbering – which are covered in this chapter – and headers and footers, page numbering, and footnotes and endnotes which are all covered in Chapter 7.

4.2 Margins and orientation

When you create a blank document the top, bottom, left and right margins are automatically set to 2.54 cm (1 inch).

To change the margins:

1 Click the **Margins** button in the **Page Setup** group.

2 Select an option from the list.

Or

3 Click **Custom Margins...**

4 Set the **Top, Bottom, Left** and/ or **Right** margins.

5 Select the **Apply to:** option

6 Click **OK**.

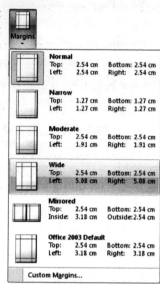

If a document has one section, the default is *Whole document*. Select this if your document is in several sections but you want the margins applied to them all.

If your document has more than one section, the default is *This section*.

This point forward inserts a new section break at the insertion point and formats the following section with your new settings.

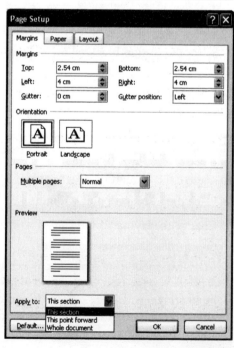

Using the ruler

You can also change the margins using the ruler. You must be in Print Layout view to do this. The blue area on the ruler indicates the margin area; the white area shows the typing area.

The top and bottom margin areas are displayed when you are at the top and bottom of the page.

To change the margins using the ruler:

1 Go into **Print Layout** view (if necessary).

2 Point to where the blue and white areas meet – the pointer changes to a double-headed arrow, and a prompt tells you which margin you are over.

• It can be tricky getting the left margin prompt as the indents are in the same area.

3 Click and drag the margin to its new position.

If you want to see the exact measurements for the margins and the distance between them, hold [**Alt**] down as you drag the margin.

When you change the margins using the ruler, they will affect only the section your insertion point is in – or the whole document if there is only one section.

To change the orientation of your pages:

1 Display the **Page Layout** tab.

2 Click **Orientation** in the **Page Setup** group.

3 Select *Portrait* or *Landscape*.

Or

1 Launch the **Page Setup** dialog box.

2 On the **Margins** tab, select the **Orientation** required.

3 Select the **Apply to...** options required.

4 Click **OK**.

4.3 Multiple page options

There are a number of options to choose from in Page Setup if you have a multi-page document.

Normal. This is the normal layout!

Mirror Margins. This changes the Left and Right margins to Inside and Outside and can be useful when printing double-sided. The inside margins mirror each other, as do the outside ones.

Gutter

Multiple page options

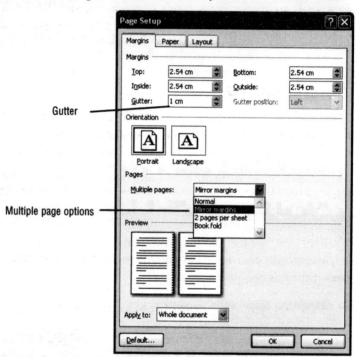

Gutters

If you are going to bind your document, you need to set a *gutter margin* to allow for the binding, either on the left or the top of the page. If the binding method will take 1.25 cm, set the gutter to 1.25 cm. This amount will be left at the edge before the left (or top) margin is calculated – the distance between the margins (i.e. the text area) is reduced automatically to allow for the gutter.

2 pages per sheet. This prints 2 pages on each sheet of paper. The paper can be portrait or landscape orientation.

Book fold. If you wish to produce a booklet, specify the page setup before you begin to enter your text and graphics. If you don't, you may find that you have to reposition objects and reformat text to get the layout required. The paper orientation is automatically set to landscape (if you haven't specified this) and the left and right margins changed to outside and inside. Two pages are printed on one side of the paper, and Word will take care of deciding which two pages so that when you fold your booklet, the pages are in the right order!

4.4 Columns

Most documents have the text in one column, running across the page from margin to margin. If you create leaflets, news-letters or advertising fliers, you may want your text to appear in several columns across the page, rather than just one.

If you want a different number of columns on different parts of a page, first divide it up using continuous section breaks.

To insert a continuous section break:

1 Place the insertion point where you want the section break.

2 Click **Break** in the **Page Setup** group.

3 Select **Continuous** from the **Section Breaks** options.

To set the number of columns:

1 Place the insertion point in the section you want to format.

2 Click **Columns** in the **Page Setup** group.

3 Select a columns layout.

Or

4 Choose **More Columns...** at the end of the **Columns** list.

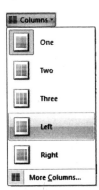

Use a preset layout or set the number of columns

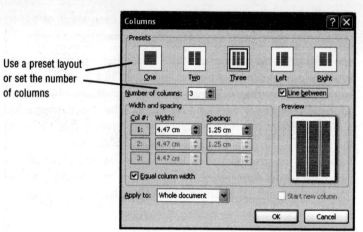

5 Set the number of columns – you can have up to 15 (portrait) or 20 (landscape) – it depends on margin settings and font size.

6 Select any other options required, e.g. **Line between** (columns), **Equal column width**.

7 Set the **Width** and **Spacing** between columns as necessary.

8 Select an **Apply to:** option.

9 Click **OK**.

When you type into a page that has multiple columns, the text flows down to the bottom of the first column, then wraps to the top of the next column. It fills the second column, then wraps to the next one and so on. You can force a column break if you don't want the text to run to the bottom of the page.

To insert a column break:

1 Place the insertion point where you want a break.

2 Click **Breaks** in the **Page Setup** group.

3 Select **Column**.

• The keyboard shortcut is **[Shift]-[Ctrl]-[Enter]**.

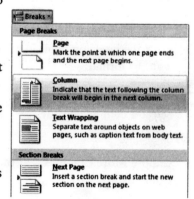

The example here has a continuous section break inserted after the heading. Section 1 is set to display one column – this allows the heading to run across the whole page. Section 2 is formatted to display 2 columns. The text has wrapped automatically at the bottom of the first column and flowed to the top of the second.

You can find out how to insert a picture in Chapter 10.

4.5   Paper size and source

Paper size

The default paper size is A4 (21 cm by 29.7 cm). If you are printing onto paper that is a different size, you should set the paper size accordingly.

To change the paper size:

1   Click the **Size** button in the **Page Setup** group.

2   Select the size from the list.

Or

3   Click **More Paper Sizes...**

4   Specify the paper size in the dialog box.

5   Set the **Apply to:** field as necessary.

6   Click **OK**.

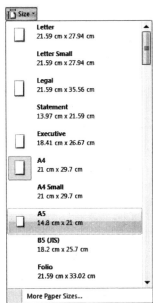

Paper source

If a printer has more than one paper tray, you may want to specify the paper source for some, or all, of your document. It may be that one of the trays contains your company letterhead stationery, or pre-printed forms. You can specify the paper source in the Page Setup dialog box, on the Paper tab.

1 Launch the **Page Setup** dialog box.

2 Display the **Paper** tab.

3 Select the **Paper source** for the **First page** and for the **Other pages** in the document or section.

4 Click **OK**.

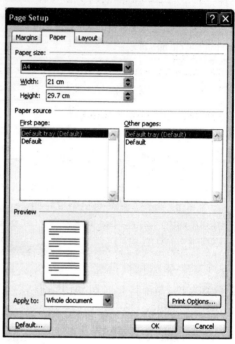

4.6 Line numbering

If you generate documents where you want to be able to reference locations within the document by line number, you can easily add line numbers down the left of your text, in whatever increment you require.

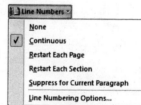

To add line numbers:

1 Click the **Line Numbers** button in the **Page Layout** group.

2 Select a line numbering option.

```
322   4.6 Line Numbering
323
324   If you generate documents where you want to be
325   able to reference locations within the document by
326   line number, you can easily add line numbers
327   down the left of your text, in whatever increment
328   you require.
329
```

If you wish to set your numbering to every 5 or 10 lines for example, you can do so in the Line Numbers dialog box.

To set line numbering options:

1 Click the **Line Numbers** button in the **Page Layout** group.

2 Select **Line Numbering Options...**

3 Click **Line Numbering...** on the **Layout** tab of the **Page Layout** dialog box.

4 Set the options required.

5 Click **OK** to close the **Line Numbers** dialog box.

6 Click **OK** to close the **Page Layout** dialog box.

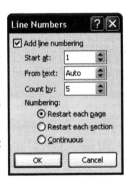

Line numbering set to 'Count by 5'

```
      When you change a layout feature an
      Word automatically inserts a section
      using the Break dialog box.

5     To insert a section break:

      1. Display the Page Layout tab
      2. Click Breaks in the Page Setup g
      3. Choose the type of Section Break
10
      Section break options

      • Next Page – inserts a section brea
        point and starts the next section at
15      next page.
```

4.7   Hyphenation

When the text reaches the right margin, it will wrap automatically to the next line. Depending on the number of characters in a word, this may result in some fairly large gaps at the right edge of the text area. If you use a lot of long words, the problem can become particularly obvious.

You can use the hyphenation options to help control the way that words wrap and split at the end of each line.

By default, no hyphenation option is selected.

To specify a hyphenation option:

1   Click the **Hyphenation** button in the **Page Setup** group.

2   Select the option required – *None*, *Automatic* or *Manual*.

♦   If you choose *Automatic*, Word will automatically hyphenate all words that fall within the hyphenation criteria.

> **Book fold**. If you wish to produce a booklet, specify the page setup by choosing Book fold *before* you begin to enter your text/graphics. If you don't you may find that you have to reposition objects and reformat text to get the layout required. The paper orientation is automatically set to landscape (if you haven't already specified this) and the left and right margins change to outside and inside margins. You must specify the number of pages that will be in your booklet in the Sheets per booklet: field. Two pages are printed on one side of the paper.

♦   If you choose *Manual*, Word will check your document and display a prompt when it encounters a word that needs a hyphenation decision. You can decide on what hyphenation action you want to take for each word.

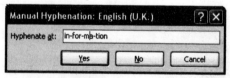

If there is more than one place that hyphenation could occur, Word will indicate where each one is.

To respond to the Manual Hyphenation dialog box:

1   Move the cursor within the **Hyphenate at:** field until you are in the position that you want to insert the hyphen.

2 Click **Yes.**

Or

* If you don't want to insert a hyphen, click **No.**

If you want to adjust the hyphenation zone (the amount of space that hyphenation occurs in at the right margin), or set a limit on the number of consecutive rows that can be hyphenated, you can customize the settings in the Hyphenation dialog box.

To customize the hyphenation options:

1 Click the **Hyphenation** button in the **Page Setup** group.

2 Select **Hyphenation Options...**

3 Set the options as required.

4 Click **OK.**

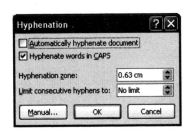

4.8   Page background

Page border

If you want to add a special effect to a page, you might like to have a look at the **Page Border** options. Borders can be very effective on menus, newsletters, programmes, invitations, etc.

To apply a page border:

1 Display the **Page Layout** tab.

2 Click the **Page Borders** button in the **Page Background** group.

3 Select the border style – use the basic line styles, or try out the **Art** options.

4 Click **OK.**

Other background options include page colour and watermark.

Page colour

If your document is going to be viewed online, you might want
to add some interest by setting a page colour. I would suggest
you keep it fairly light, so that people can read your text easily.
If you want to print your page out with a coloured background,
it may be cheaper to buy coloured paper!

To change the page colour:

1 Click the **Page Color** button in the **Page
Background** group.

2 Select a colour.

Or

♦ Choose **More Colors...** or **Fill Effects...**
and explore the options available.

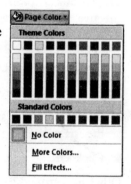

Watermarks

A watermark is the 'washed out' image or text that you often see behind the text in company documents, e.g. Draft or Confidential.

To add a watermark:

1 Click the **Watermark** button in the **Page Background** group.

2 Select **Custom Watermark...**

Text watermark

3 Select the **Text watermark** option.

4 Type your text in the Text field.

5 Set the other options and click **OK**.

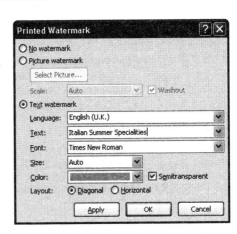

Picture watermark

6 Select the **Picture watermark** option.

7 Click **Select Picture...**

8 Locate and select the picture.

9 Set the scaling option – **Auto** usually works fine.

10 Select or deselect **Washout** as required and click **OK**.

To remove a watermark:

1 Click the **Watermark** button in the **Page Background** group.

2 Select **Remove Watermark**.

4.9   Vertical alignment of text

By default, text is aligned to the top of the page. If you are producing a menu, flier or invitation, you may prefer to centre it vertically, with an equal amount of space above and below. The vertical alignment is controlled from the Layout tab in the Page Setup dialog box.

To set the vertical alignment:

1   Launch the **Page Setup** dialog box.

2   Select the **Layout** tab.

3   Set the vertical alignment – top, centred, justified or bottom.

4   Click **OK**.

Summary

This chapter has considered some of the features that control the appearance of your page. We have discussed:

* Sections and the different types of breaks

* Margins

* Orientation

* Multiple page options

* Columns

* Paper size and source

* Line numbers

* Hyphenation

* Page borders

* Page colour and watermarks

* Vertical alignment.

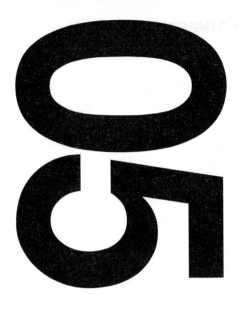

05

styles

In this chapter you will learn:

- how to use Quick Styles
- about working with Style Sets
- how to create and modify styles
- about the default formatting options

5.1   Putting on the style

What is a style?

A style is simply a named collection of formatting options. There are two kinds:

* **Character styles** where the formatting options are taken from the Font dialog box. These styles can be applied to any amount of text, from a single character to the whole document.

* **Paragraph styles** where the options can be a combination of font and paragraph formatting. These can only be applied to whole paragraphs.

Why should you use styles?

Speed – Once you've collected your formatting options into a style, you can then apply the style to your text, rather than apply each formatting option individually. If you have more than a couple of options stored in your style, it is usually quicker to apply a style than apply each option individually.

Consistency – If you collect the formatting options you want to use into a style, then apply it to your text and paragraphs, the formatting throughout your document will be more consistent.

* Word's Heading styles 1–9 make it easier to work with long documents. They are used in Outline view (see 7.10) and when generating a table of contents (see 7.12).

You've been using styles since you started using Word – but you probably didn't notice. The formatting that your font and paragraph have are determined by a style called Normal.

The default Normal style is a paragraph style that is left aligned and in single line spacing. The characters are formatted using the Calibri font, size 11 (unless you have changed it).

5.2 Quick Styles

Each document has several styles already set up for you to use. The Quick Styles are in the Styles group on the Home tab.

More

• Click the **More** button to display the Quick Styles gallery.

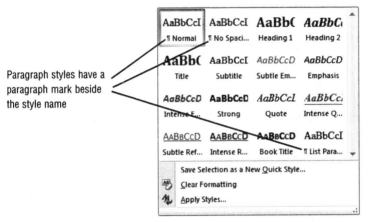

Paragraph styles have a paragraph mark beside the style name

You can apply styles in the same way as any other formatting:

To apply a style to new text:

1 Select the style required.

2 Type in your text.

3 Press [**Enter**].

To apply a style to existing text:

1 Select the text.

2 Click the **More** button to display the Quick Styles gallery.

3 Choose the style from those available.

- If you have Live Preview enabled (see page 50) when you move the pointer over each style, you can see the effect that it will create before you actually select it.

Quick effects using Quick Styles

The layout of the menu has been reformatted quickly by applying the:

- *Title* style to 'Lunch Menu'.
- *Subtitle* style to the date.
- *Intense Emphasis* style to the body of the menu.

Apply Styles

If the style you want is not displayed in the Quick Styles gallery, you can display the Apply Styles dialog box and select the style you want from the list.

To use the Apply Styles dialog box:

1 Press **[Ctrl]-[Shift]-[S]**.

Or

♦ Click **Apply Styles...** at the bottom of the **Quick Styles** gallery.

2 Scroll through and select a style.

Or

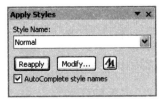

♦ Start to type the style name into the **Style Name:** field.

3 Click **Reapply** and close the **Apply Styles** dialog box.

5.3 Style sets

The Quick Styles are part of the template that you based your document on (e.g. the *Blank Document* template). You can change the formatting of your entire document by choosing a different style set. Once you have selected a set, the Quick Styles gallery displays its styles. You can customize a style set by changing the colour theme or the font used, to vary the effect.

To change the document style set:

1 Click **Change Styles** in the **Styles** group.

2 Select **Style Set**.

3 Click on the set you want to use.

As you experiment with styles, you might decide that you want to return to the original styles that your document used.

1 Click the **Change Styles** button.

2 Select **Style Set**.

3 Click **Reset to Quick Styles from Template**.

You can customize the settings in the style set by changing the colour theme used or by selecting a different font.

To change the colour theme:

1 Click the **Change Styles** button.

2 Point to **Colors**.

3 Select a theme.

To change the font:

1 Click **Change Styles**.

2 Point to **Fonts**.

3 Select a font.

◆ If you display your font list, the Theme Fonts will be displayed at the top of the list.

Set as Default

You can change the default style set used by your documents, then every new one you create using that template will have your preferred style set and options active automatically.

To set the default style set:

1 Select the **Style Set** you want to use.

2 Select the **Color** theme and **Font** options.

3 Click the **Change Styles** button and choose **Set as Default**.

5.4 Styles task pane

As an alternative to using the Quick Styles gallery, you can select styles from the Styles task pane.

To use the style list:

1 Click the launcher button at the bottom right of the Styles group to display the task pane.

2 Select the style required.

♦ A description of the formatting in the style is displayed when you point to it.

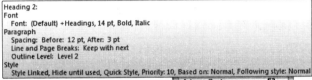

3 Close the task pane when you have finished using it.

♦ To have the styles previewed in the task pane, select the **Show Preview** checkbox at the bottom.

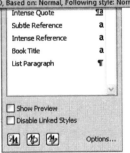

Style Inspector

If you want to check what styles are applied to selected text, you can use the Style Inspector. This will display details of its paragraph and character formatting styles.

To use the Style Inspector:

1 Position the insertion point within the text you want to check.

2 Click the **Style Inspector** button at the bottom of the Styles task pane.

Other styles

Word has many different styles stored in each document template. The styles that are available to you in any one document are the ones that are stored in the template on which it is based. Even then, the only styles displayed by default are those from the Recommended list. You can display the other styles available to the document in the Styles Pane Options dialog box.

To open the Options dialog box:

1 Display the **Styles** task pane.

2 Click **Options...** at the bottom of it.

3 Select the styles you want to show in the **Select styles to show:** list.

4 Click **OK**.

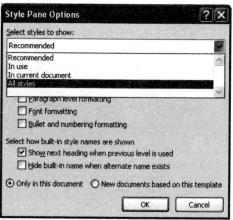

5.5 Creating a new style

You can always create your own styles if you wish. It may be that you always want a specific set of formatting options applied to the text 'Key Fact' throughout your document. You could create a style for this and apply it as necessary.

To create a new style:

1 Format some text in your document using the formats you want in your style.

2 Select the text.

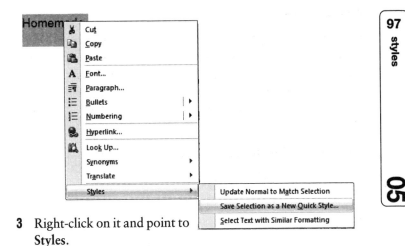

3 Right-click on it and point to **Styles.**

Or

- Display the Quick Styles gallery.

4 Click on **Save Selection as a New Quick Style...**

5 Give your style a name.

6 Click **OK.**

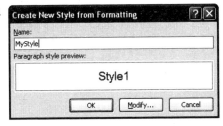

- Your style will appear in the Quick Styles gallery and the Styles task pane.

- You can create a style from the Styles task pane – click the **New Style** button at the bottom to display the dialog box.

5.6 Modifying an existing style

You can change the formatting in either the Word styles or your own styles. If you change the formatting in a style, all text within your document that has that style applied to it will adopt the modified formatting options.

To modify a style:

1 Right-click on the style in the Quick Styles gallery.

Or

♦ Click the arrow beside a selected style in the task pane.

2 Choose **Modify...**

3 In the **Modify Style** dialog box, make the changes required.

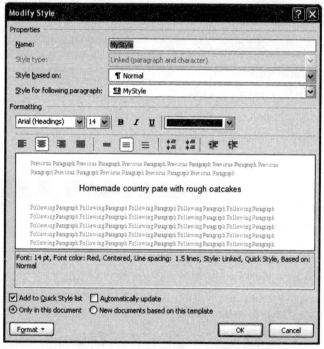

Click the **Format** button to access more formatting options

4 Set the options using the checkboxes and radio buttons.

♦ **Add to Quick Style list** displays the style in the Quick Styles gallery.

♦ **Automatically update** updates a style automatically if you apply manual formatting to text formatted with that style.

♦ **Only in this document** limits the effect of changing your style to the current document.

- **New documents based on this template** updates the style and will be available to all documents based on the template.

5 Click **OK**.

5.7 Removing and deleting styles

Having your styles in the Quick Style Gallery is useful as it gives you quick access to them at all times. However, you may prefer not to have all your styles in the gallery.

To remove a style from the gallery:

1 Right-click on it.

2 Select **Remove from Quick Style Gallery**.

Removing a style from the gallery does not delete it – you will still be able to access it from the Styles task pane.

If you want to delete a style, you can do so from the Styles task pane.

To delete a style:

1 Display the **Styles** task pane.

2 Click the drop-down arrow to the right of the style.

3 Choose **Delete** *Stylename...*

4 Click **Yes** at the prompt to confirm the deletion, or **No** if you have changed your mind.

If you delete a style that has been applied to some text in your document, the text picks up its formatting from the Normal style.

- You can delete your own styles, but you cannot delete those that are pre-set in Word.

5.8 Style management

When you create a new document, the styles available to you are its recommended styles. You can edit the recommended style lists, or move styles from one template to another, and perform other style management tasks from the Organizer dialog box.

To manage your styles:

1 Display the **Styles** task pane.

2 Click the **Manage Styles** button 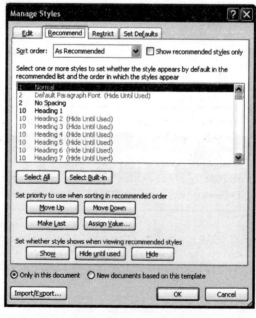 at the bottom of the pane.

There are four tabs from which you can manage your styles.

♦ **Edit:** Used to modify existing styles, create new styles and change the sort order of styles.

♦ **Recommend:** Edit the Recommended styles list from this tab – specify which styles to show and which to hide.

♦ **Restrict:** You can set restrictions on the editing options available to users when a document is protected on this tab.

♦ **Set Defaults:** Set the default font options.

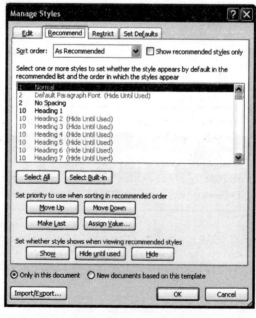

The tab you are probably most interested in if you wish to change the list of default styles available to you is Recommend.

If you have created a style and want to copy it to a template so that it is automatically available in other documents, or if you wish to copy a style from a different template to the current document, you could use the Organizer dialog box.

To import or export styles:

1   Click **Import/Export...** in the **Manage Styles** dialog box.

2   In the **Organizer** dialog box, on the **Styles** tab, you will have two lists of styles – the list on the left are those in the current document, those on the right are those in the template the document was based on.

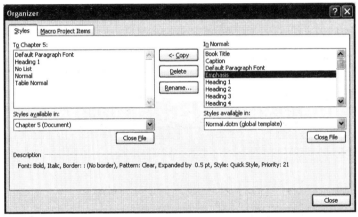

If you don't want to work with the files that are currently open, you can close either or both in the Organizer dialog box, and open the files required.

•   When you close a file here, the **Close File** button becomes the **Open File** button. Click this to locate and open the file you want to use.

•   When you open a file, the default file type listed in the **Open** dialog box is *Templates*. It you want to open a document, change the **Files of type** field to *Word documents*.

05

To copy a style from one list to another:

♦ Select the style and click **Copy**.

To delete a style:

♦ Select the style and click **Delete**.

To rename a style:

1 Select the style.

2 Click **Rename...**

3 Enter a new name.

4 Click **OK**.

Summary

In this chapter we have looked at Styles, and discussed how they can help speed up your formatting routines, and also help ensure that your document maintains a consistent look. We have considered:

♦ Applying styles using the Quick Styles gallery

♦ Changing the Style set used in a document

♦ Customizing a Style set by changing the colour theme and/or font

♦ Specifying a Style set as the default

♦ Using the Style task pane

♦ The Style Inspector

♦ Creating your own styles

♦ Modifying styles

♦ Removing styles from the Quick Styles gallery

♦ Deleting styles

♦ Style management.

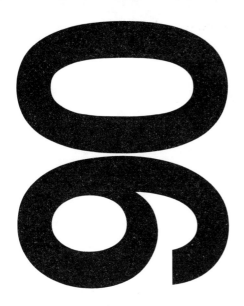

06

tables

In this chapter you will learn:

- how to create tables
- how to manipulate tables
- how to sort the data in tables
- about calculations in tables
- how to create a chart from data in a table

6.1 Create a table

There are several ways to create a table, but they all start from the Insert tab on the Ribbon.

To create a table:

1 Display the **Insert** tab.

2 Click **Table** in the **Tables** group.

3 Drag over the grid to set the size of the table.

4 Release the mouse button – an empty table will be displayed on your page.

Or

1 Click **Table** in the **Tables** group and then click **Insert Table...**

2 Specify the number of columns and rows in the **Insert Table** dialog box.

3 Click **OK**.

To draw a table on your page:

1 Click **Table** in the **Tables** group on the **Insert** tab and then click **Draw Table**.

◆ The **Draw Table** button is automatically selected. (It is in the **Draw Borders** group on the **Design** tab in the Table Tools.)

Table jargon

Tables are arranged in a grid, consisting of rows and columns. Where a row and column intersect, you get a rectangular area called a cell.

		Column	
Row		Cell	

2 Click and drag on your slide to draw a rectangle the size you want your table to be.

3 Click and drag to draw in rows and columns as required.

4 Switch the Draw Table feature off – click the **Draw Table** button or press [Esc].

If you draw a line in the wrong place, remove it with the Eraser.

To remove a line:

1 Select the **Eraser** button.

2 Click on the line with the tip of the Eraser pointer.

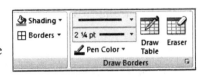

3 Deselect the Eraser – click the button again, or press [Esc].

Use the buttons in the Draw Borders group to specify the Line style, Line weight and Pen colour for your borders when drawing your table.

• It doesn't matter which method you use to create the table – once you have it on your page you can format it and manipulate it in many different ways.

Table Tools

The Table Tools are displayed automatically when the insertion point is inside a table.

Design tab

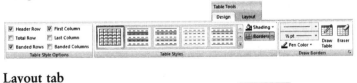

Layout tab

6.2 Basic table skills

To enter text or data, go to the cell then just type! Text will automatically wrap once it reaches the right edge of the cell, and the row will deepen to accommodate it. You can format the text or data in the cells, using the normal formatting commands.

◆ Text and numbers automatically align to the left of a cell.

◆ The table has inside and outside borders applied to the cells automatically.

Table navigation

You can move around a table using the keyboard or the mouse:

◆ Click in the cell you want to move to.

Or

◆ Press [**Tab**] to move forward to the next cell.

◆ Press [**Shift**] – [**Tab**] to move back to the previous cell.

If you press [**Tab**] when the insertion point is in the last cell in the last row of your table, a new row is created.

Selection techniques

To select the current cell, column or row, or the whole table:

1 Click the arrow to the right of **Select** in the **Table** group on the **Layout** tab of the Table Tools.

2 Select the option required.

Or

◆ **To select a cell:** point just within the left cell border (the pointer should be a black arrow) and click.

◆ **To select a column:** point at the top of the column (the pointer should be a black arrow pointing down) and click.

◆ **To select a row:** point to the left of the row (the pointer should be a black arrow pointing to the right) and click.

- To select any block of cells: drag over them.

- To select adjacent rows or columns: click and drag in the selector areas to the left of a row or above a column.

Row heights and column widths

When you create a table, each column is the same width, and the table stretches across the page. When entering text into a cell, the cell will deepen automatically to accommodate the text.

To adjust a row height:

- Drag the lower border up or down.

To adjust a column width:

- Drag the right border right or left.

Or

- Set the **Height** and **Width** required in the **Cell Size** group on the **Layout** tab.

Cafés and pubs – Scottish Borders		
Address	**Notes**	**Cost**
Old Mill Inn Old Mill Lane Melrose	Delightful retreat in the Scottish borders. Food available from 10 am through until 10 pm. Excellent lunches and evening meals. Accommodation available. Working waterwheel, herb garden and riverside walks.	Lunches from £5. Dinner from £12.50. Dinner, Bed and Breakfast: £38 per head.
Kathy's Kitchen 12 High Street Duns	Excellent family run coffee shop. Soup, baked potatoes, sandwiches, etc. available all day. Delicious home baking.	Various.

To reset the row heights so that each row is the same:

1 Select the rows.

2 Click **Distribute Rows** in the **Cell Size** group.

To reset the column widths so that each column is the same:

1 Select the columns.

2 Click **Distribute Columns** in the **Cell Size** group.

There are also **AutoFit** options in this group, so that you can get your table to fit around the cell contents automatically, or fit within the width of the window or adopt a fixed width. Experiment with them to see how they affect your columns.

Table width

If you want your table to be a specific width, set it in the Table Properties dialog box.

To set the table size:

1 Click **Properties** in the **Table** group on the Layout tab.

2 Select the **Table** tab in the dialog box.

3 Select the **Preferred width** checkbox.

4 Enter the table width required.

5 Click **OK**.

Inserting rows and columns

Adding rows to the end of a table is done automatically – just press [Tab] when the insertion point is in the last cell of the table and a new row is added. If you need to add or delete rows or columns anywhere else in your table, use the buttons in the Rows & Columns group on the Layout tab.

To insert rows:

1 Position the insertion point anywhere in the row above or below the one you want to insert.

2 Click **Insert Above** or **Insert Below** in the **Rows & Columns** group.

To insert columns:

1 Position the insertion point anywhere in the column to the right or the left of the one you want to insert.

Cafés and pubs – Scottish Borders			
Contact	**Address**	**Notes**	**Cost**
Jill Syme	Old Mill Inn Old Mill Lane Melrose	Delightful retreat in the Scottish borders. Food available from 10 am through until 10 pm. Excellent lunches and evening meals. Accommodation available. Working waterwheel, herb garden and riverside walks.	Lunches from £5. Dinner from £12.50. Dinner, Bed and Breakfast: £38 per head.
Kathy or Anna	Kathy's Kitchen 12 High Street Duns	Excellent family run coffee shop. Soup, baked potatoes, sandwiches, etc. available all day. Delicious home baking.	Various.

Table Properties dialog box

Most aspects of a table's size or formatting can be found in the Table Properties dialog box. In addition to specifying row, column and cell attributes, you can also set alignment and text wrapping for the whole table. If you want to centre your table horizontally on the page, or get text to wrap around the side of it – this is where you can specify these options!

2 Click the **Insert Left** or **Insert Right** button in the **Rows &
Columns** group.

Delete cells, columns, rows or table

1 Position the insertion point anywhere
within the cell, column, row or table you
wish to delete.

2 Click the **Delete** button and select a **Delete**
option.

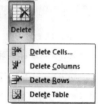

Gridlines

The gridlines are the visible boundaries that surround the cells
in your table. They can be very useful as they let you see the
boundaries of your table cells. They do not print out.

If your table has borders applied to it (as is the default) the
gridlines are hidden. If you remove the borders from a table,
and don't have gridlines displayed, the table will 'disappear' –
and you will only be aware of its presence if you have something
typed into it.

To toggle the display of the gridlines:

♦ Click [⊞ **View Gridlines**] in the **Table** group on the **Layout** tab.

6.3 Cell formatting

Font/character formatting is applied using the Font formatting
commands, in the same way as you would apply them to text in
any other area of your document. These next formatting options can be applied to the cells themselves, and are especially
for table layout.

Alignment options

You can align your text or data within a cell using the Alignment tools. The default alignment is Align Left and Align Top.

- The horizontal alignment options are Left, Centre or Right.
- The vertical options are Top, Centre Vertically or Bottom.

To change the alignment options of your cell(s):

1 Select the cell(s).

2 Click a button in the **Alignment** group.

Text Direction

Text normally displays horizontally within a cell – from left to right. However, you might want to change the text direction for some cells – you will often see the text direction changed in column heading cells where the entry is quite long.

The options are left-to-right, top-to-bottom and bottom-to-top.

To change the text direction:

- Click the **Text Direction** button in the Alignment group to cycle through the options, and stop at the one required.

Cell Margins

The cell margins are the amount of space between the edge of a cell and the cell contents.

To change the margin:

1 Select the cell(s) and click the **Cell Margins** button.

2 Set the cell margins in the **Table Options** dialog box.

3 Select the **Default cell spacing** checkbox if you want to leave a space between cells, and specify the amount.

4 If you want your cells to resize automatically, select the checkbox.

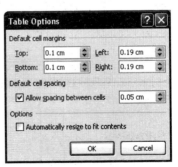

5 Click **OK**.

Merge Cells

This feature is sometimes used to combine cells in the heading row of a table if you want an entry running all the way across the table.

* Select the cells to be merged and click **Merge Cells** in the **Merge** group.

Cells merged horizontally			
Merged vertically over two rows	Merged horizontally and vertically over three columns and two rows		

Split Cells

You can split cells that have been merged, or you can divide a single cell up into more cells by splitting it.

1 Select the cell(s) that you want to split.

2 Click **Split Cells**.

3 Specify the number of columns and rows to split the cell into.

4 If you want the resulting cells to be the same width/height, select the **Merge cells before split** checkbox.

5 Click **OK**.

* The merge and split cells feature is often very useful when designing forms.

Student Test Results												
	Chemistry			English			Computing			French		
Student ID	Winter	Spring	Summer	Winter	Spring	Summer	Winter	Spring	Summer	Winter	Spring	Summer
PR4	45	52	56	65	58	62	55	60	53	62	53	64
DD14	76	70	72	70	72	69	74	68	71	71	65	74
ST3	65	68	72	81	75	84	68	67	64	68	70	68
RR3	35	42	51	64	62	60	48	52	56	55	58	62

Split Table

As well as merging and splitting cells, you can split a table horizontally if necessary.

To split a table:

1 Position the insertion point in the row below where you want the split.

2 Click **Split Table** in the **Merge** group.

Cell borders

When you create a table, the default is for it to have ½ pt, black borders applied inside and outside. You can edit them or remove them using the Borders commands on the Design tab.

The Line Style, Line Weight and Pen Color are in the Draw Borders group, Borders (where you can specify where you want the border in relation to the selected cells) is in the Table Styles group.

To format the borders:

1 Select the cell(s).

2 Choose **Line Style, Line Weight** and/or **Pen Color**.

3 Click the arrow to the right of the **Borders** button.

4 Select the position of the border relative to the selected cells.

Cafés and pubs – Scottish Borders			
Contact	**Address**	**Notes**	**Cost**
Jill Syme	Old Mill Inn Old Mill Lane Melrose	Delightful retreat in the Scottish borders. Food available from 10 am through until 10 pm. Excellent lunches and evening meals. Accommodation available. Working waterwheel, herb garden and riverside walks.	Lunches from £5. Dinner from £12.50. Dinner, Bed and Breakfast: £38 per head.
Kathy or Anna	Kathy's Kitchen 12 High Street Duns	Excellent family run coffee shop. Soup, baked potatoes, sandwiches, etc. available all day. Delicious home baking.	Various.

Convert table to text

Having set up your data in a table, if you then want the data but not in a table layout, you can convert the table to text.

To convert a table to text:

1 Select the table.

2 Click the ⬛ Convert to Text button in the **Data** group.

3 At the dialog box, select the separator character to use.

4 Click **OK**.

6.4   Table styles

As an alternative to manually formatting your tables, you can create a professional look very quickly by using the table styles.

To apply a style:

1 Click anywhere within your table.

2 Scroll through the styles, or click the **More** button to display the Styles gallery.

────── More

Table Styles

3 Select a style. The shading and border effects stored in the style are applied to your table.

Cafés and pubs – Scottish Borders			
Contact	**Address**	**Notes**	**Cost**
Jill Syme	Old Mill Inn Old Mill Lane Melrose	Delightful retreat in the Scottish borders. Food available from 10 am through until 10 pm. Excellent lunches and evening meals. Accommodation available. Working waterwheel, herb garden and riverside walks.	Lunches from £5. Dinner from £12.50. Dinner, Bed and Breakfast: £38 per head.
Kathy or Anna	Kathy's Kitchen 12 High Street Duns	Excellent family run coffee shop. Soup, baked potatoes, sandwiches, etc. available all day. Delicious home baking.	Various.

Once a table style has been applied, you can customize it:

* Modify the shading and border options using the Shading and Borders buttons.

Or

* Switch individual elements of the style on and off, using the **Table Style Options** checkboxes to the left of the styles.

☑ Header Row	☑ First Column
☐ Total Row	☐ Last Column
☑ Banded Rows	☐ Banded Columns
Table Style Options	

6.5 Sorting data in tables

Tables are often used to display a list of data – names and phone numbers, stock items, student names, etc. Lists often need to be manipulated and sorted into different orders – and this is easily done in a table.

The table below could be sorted in a number of different ways:

* On a single column, e.g. *Country* or *Town* order.

* An alphabetical listing on *Surname* then *First name* order.

* A list in *Country*, *Town* then *Surname* order.

You can sort on up to three levels at a time.

First name	Surname	Address	Town	Country
Jill	Wilson	22 High Street	Birmingham	England
Robert	Adamson	4a Mill Wynd	Greenlaw	Scotland
Malcolm	Simpson	Western Cottage	Perth	Scotland
Alison	Birch	10 High Croft	Birmingham	England
Carol	Adamson	Summerfield Way	Perth	Scotland
Rebecca	Jackson	102 Lower Lane	Cardiff	Wales
Gordon	Peterson	13 Grange Loan	Edinburgh	Scotland
Penny	Fullerton	82 All Saints Way	Cork	Ireland
James	Russell	2a Ferry Lane	Ascot	England

To perform a sort:

1 Place the insertion point anywhere in the table.

2 Click the **Sort** button in the **Data** group on the **Layout** tab.

Sort

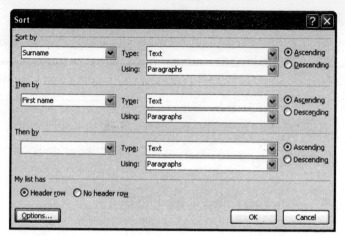

3 At the **Sort** dialog box specify the first level, e.g. *Surname*, then the second, e.g. *First name*, then the third if required. You do not have to sort on three fields – for a simple sort, just specify the first level of sort.

4 Click **OK**.

Note that:

• You can sort in ascending or descending order.

• Different types of data can be sorted – Text, Number or Date – in an appropriate order for the type.

• The table may or may not have a Header row. The first row in a table usually contains column headings. If the first row is to be sorted along with the others, select **No header row**.

First name	Surname	Address	Town	Country
Carol	Adamson	Summerfield Way	Perth	Scotland
Robert	Adamson	4a Mill Wynd	Greenlaw	Scotland
Alison	Birch	10 High Croft	Birmingham	England
Penny	Fullerton	82 All Saints Way	Cork	Ireland
Rebecca	Jackson	102 Lower Lane	Cardiff	Wales
Gordon	Peterson	13 Grange Loan	Edinburgh	Scotland
James	Russell	2a Ferry Lane	Ascot	England
Malcolm	Simpson	Western Cottage	Perth	Scotland
Jill	Wilson	22 High Street	Birmingham	England

Table sorted by Surname and then by First name.

6.6 Header rows

If your table is big, and runs to more than one page, it is often useful to have the header rows in your table repeat at the top of each page. That way, those reading it will be reminded of what data is in what column.

To get rows to repeat at the top of each page:

1 Select the rows you want to repeat – usually row one and/or two of your table.

2 Click [🗒 Repeat Header Rows] in the **Data** group.

The selected rows are repeated at the top of each page.

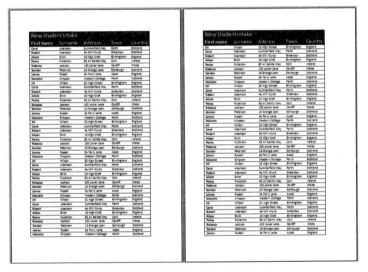

To remove the Header Row Repeat condition:

1 Select the header rows again.

2 Click [🗒 Repeat Header Rows] in the **Data** group.

6.7 Simple sums

You can do some calculations in a table, e.g. sum a range of cells, or work out the average, or count the number of entries. If you use Excel as well as Word, it's often easier to insert a worksheet into your document (see Chapter 12), and use Excel's functions. However, if you want to do calculations in Word, here's how.

To add a range of cells:

1 Position the insertion point inside the cell you want to contain a formula.

2 Click 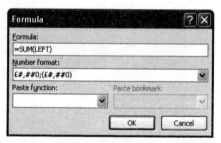 in the **Data** group.

3 If the formula suggested is not the one you want, delete it and enter the right formula.

4 If you want a specific number format, e.g. currency, select it from the Number Format list.

5 Click **OK**.

Formula	? X
<u>F</u>ormula:	
=SUM(LEFT)	
<u>N</u>umber format:	
£#,##0;(£#,##0)	▼
Paste f<u>u</u>nction:	Paste bookmark:
▼	▼
	OK Cancel

The formulas are entered as fields in your table.

Sales Figures (in £s)			
	January	February	March	TOTAL
Bill	12,300	10,500	9,750	32,550
Ann	14,500	12,500	10,750	37,750
Bert	10,750	14,500	13,500	38,750
TOTAL	37,550	37,500	34,000	109,050

If you change any of the figures that feed your formulas, the result is not updated automatically. Some of the figures have been changed in the table below, but the total row and column remain unchanged.

Sales Figures (in £s)			
	January	February	March	TOTAL
Bill	99,300	10,500	9,750	32,550
Ann	14,500	32,500	10,750	37,750
Bert	10,750	14,500	53,500	38,750
TOTAL	37,550	37,500	34,000	109,050

To update all the cells with formulas in them:

1 Select the entire table.

2 Press [F9].

Sales Figures (in £s)			
	January	February	March	TOTAL
Bill	99,300	10,500	9,750	119,550
Ann	14,500	32,500	10,750	57,750
Bert	10,750	14,500	53,500	78,750
TOTAL	124,550	57,500	74,000	256,050

- To update a single field: click into it and press [F9].
- To toggle the display of all the field codes: press [Alt]-[F9].
- To toggle the display of a specific field code: click into the field and press [Shift]-[F9].

The cells in the table are identified by cell addresses (or names) as they are in a spreadsheet. The first column is A, the second is B, etc. Rows are numbered 1, 2, 3, etc. A cell's address is derived from its column and row, e.g. A6, B7, D2. These addresses can be used in the formulas.

Acceptable formulas include:

=Sum (above)	
=Sum (left)	
=A7+B6	Add the value in A7 to that in B6
=A1-B2	Subtract the value in B2 from that in A1
=A3/B6	Divide the value in A3 by that in B6
=A4*B4	Multiply the value in A4 by that in B4
=Sum(A1:A6)	Add the range of cells from A1 to A6

=Min(A3,A7,A11)	Find the smallest value in these three separate cells.
=Count(B7:B14)	Find how many numbers there are in the range from B7 to B14

Check out Formulas in the online Help for more information.

Summary

In this chapter we have discussed using tables to lay out your document. We have looked at:

• Creating tables

• Navigation and selection techniques

• Table properties

• Inserting and deleting rows and columns

• Formatting rows, columns and cells

• Merging and splitting cells

• Borders and shading

• Table styles

• Sorting table data

• Performing calculations within tables.

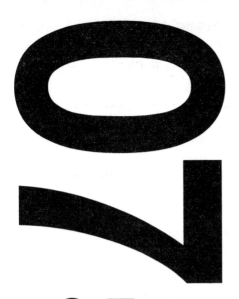

07
multi-page documents

In this chapter you will learn:

- about page breaks, headers and footers, and bookmarks
- how to use the Document Map
- about Outline and Master Document view
- how to create a table of contents and an index

7.1 Controlling page breaks

Page breaks are inserted automatically when the text reaches the end of a page. You can set a variety of pagination options in the Format Paragraph dialog box.

To specify Page break options:

1 Click the dialog box launcher at the bottom of the **Paragraph** group on the **Home** tab.

2 Select the **Line and Page Breaks** tab.

3 Select the **Pagination** options.

4 Click **OK**.

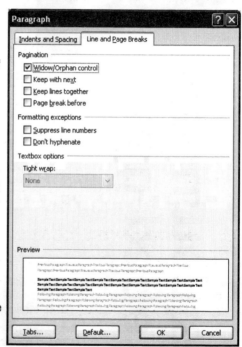

Widow/Orphan control prevents Word from printing a single last line of a paragraph at the top of a page (widow), or a single first line at the bottom of a page (orphan).

Keep with next prevents a page break between the selected paragraph and the following one.

Keep lines together prevents a page break within a paragraph.

Page break before inserts a manual page break before the selected paragraph.

In Draft view a dotted line appears across your screen when an automatic page break occurs.

In Print layout view, the insertion point moves to the top of the next page when an automatic page break occurs.

Manual page breaks

If you need to, you can force a page break before you fill a page with text, rather than wait for automatic pagination to occur.

To insert a manual page break:

* Hold down [Ctrl] and press [Enter].

In Normal view, if formatting (non-printing) characters are displayed, a dotted line will appear across your screen with the text 'Page Break' in the middle of it.

If you are in Print Layout view, the insertion point moves to the top of the next page.

* You can insert a manual page break from the **Page Layout** tab. Choose **Page Break** from the **Breaks** list.

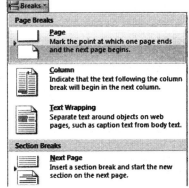

To remove a manual page break:

1 Select the page break.

2 Press [Delete].

7.2 Headers and footers

In multi-page documents headers and footers are often used for things like the author's or company name, report title or page numbers (imagine dropping a pile of unnumbered pages!). The header and footer areas are within the top and bottom margins.

You can choose to have the headers and footers:

* The same on every page (this is the default option).

* Different for the first page of your document.

* Different on odd and even pages.

To create a header or footer:

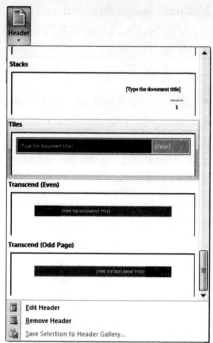

1 Click the **Header** (or **Footer**) button in the **Header & Footer** group on the **Insert** tab.

2 Scroll through the list of header/footer styles.

3 Select a style from the list.

4 Click on the content holders and enter the details required.

5 Click into the main text area to close the header and footer when you have finished.

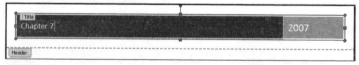

If you prefer the more traditional layout for your header or footer:

1 Choose the Blank (3 columns) style.

• Note the centre tab and the right tab on the ruler in the content holders to help you align your entries.

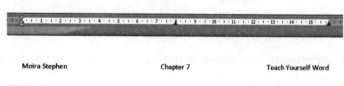

2 Click on a content holder and enter your header or footer information (if you don't want something in all three areas, right-click on the content holder and remove it).

3 Close the header or footer area.

To edit the text:

1 Click the **Header** or **Footer** button in the **Header & Footer** group.

2 Choose **Edit Header** or **Edit Footer**.

3 Make the amendments required.

4 Close the header or footer area.

To change the built-in style:

If you are in the header or footer area you can change the styles to see the effect on your document. You may need to re-enter your text if you change the style used.

1 Click the **Header** or **Footer** button.

2 Choose a style from the list.

To remove a Header or Footer:

1 Click the **Header** or **Footer** button.

2 Choose **Remove Header/Footer**.

Navigation tools

Once in the header or footer area, use the navigation buttons to move from header to footer, header to header, or footer to footer (if your document contains more than one section).

To move to the footer:

♦ Click the **Go to Footer** button in the **Navigation** group.

To move to the header:

♦ Click the **Go to Header** button in the **Navigation** group.

If your document is divided into sections, use the **Next Section/ Previous Section** buttons to move between the sections.

Different first page

The first page in a document is often a title page, and you might not want the headers and footers that appear on the other pages to be displayed on this.

To specify a different first page:

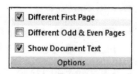

1 Select the **Different First Page** check-box in the **Options** group in the **Header & Footer** tab.

* The header area on the first page of your document will display a First Page Header area, and the footer will have a similar First Page Footer area.

2 Select a style and/or enter the text, page numbering, etc. as required into the First Page Header or Footer area (if you want nothing displayed, leave them empty). Anything entered here will be displayed on the first page only.

* To move to the header or footer that will affect the other pages in your document click the **Next Section** button.

* To return to the First Page Header or Footer, click the **Previous Section** button.

Different Odd & Even pages

You can also opt to have different headers and footers on odd and even pages – select the **Different Odd & Even Pages** checkbox in the **Options** group to activate this option. When you use the Next Section/Previous Section buttons the header and footer areas will indicate whether you are on an even page or an odd page.

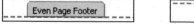

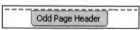

Sections

If a document is divided up into sections, you can have different headers and footers for each, e.g. Chapter 1, Chapter 2, 3, etc. Within each section you can also have different first page, or different odd and even page options selected.

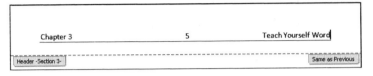

Link to Previous

The Header or Footer area will indicate which section you are in. By default, each section is linked to the previous one – indicated by the **Same as Previous** tab. To break the link between the two, click the **Link to Previous** button in the Navigation group. You can then set different headers and/or footers for each section as required.

7.3 Page numbers

Some header and footer styles have page numbering built into them. You can also number your pages without having selected a header or footer. If the only thing that you want in the header or footer area is a page number, that is all you need to add!

DO NOT be tempted to type a number into the header or footer area if you want to insert a page number – you will end up with the same number repeated on every page! Use the Page Number button in the Header & Footer group.

1 Display the **Insert** tab, and click **Page Number** in the **Header & Footer** group.

2 Click **Top of Page, Bottom of Page** or **Page Margins** to specify where you want the page numbers to appear.

3 Choose a page numbering style from the gallery.

- If you are already in the Header or Footer area, there is a **Page Number** button in the **Header & Footer** group.

Number format

Page numbering is normally formatted as 1, 2, 3, 4, etc.

To change the page numbering format:

1 Click the **Format Page Number...** option in the **Page Number** drop-down list.

2 Choose a **Number format**.

3 Specify any other options required, e.g. whether or not numbering continues from previous section, or the number to start from.

4 Click **OK**.

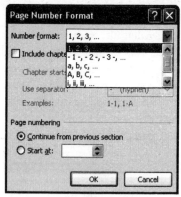

7.4 Moving through a long document

You probably use the scroll bars to move through your document most of the time. There are some other methods you might like to experiment with if you work with longer documents.

To go to the top of the previous page:

- Press [Ctrl]-[Page Up] or click the **Previous Page** button at the bottom of the vertical scroll bar.

To go to the top of the next page:

- Press [Ctrl]-[Page Down] or click the **Next Page** button at the bottom of the vertical scroll bar.

To go to the top of the document:

◆ Press [**Ctrl**]-[**Home**].

To go to the end of the document:

◆ Press [**Ctrl**]-[**End**].

To go to a specific page:

1 Double-click the page number indicator Page: 7 at the left end of the Status bar.

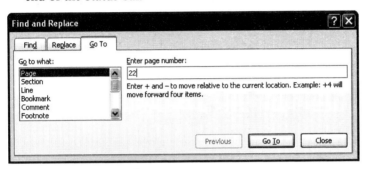

2 Enter the page number to go to.

3 Click **Go To**.

4 Click **Close**.

Or

◆ Click and drag the elevator on the vertical scrollbar – a prompt appears to tell you which page you're at. Release the button when you reach the one required.

Live word count   Words: 2,591

If you write papers, reports or essays and the word count is important, you'll love this! The Status bar displays the number of words in your document. It updates as you work – so you know exactly how many words you have – all the time! If the word count isn't displayed, right-click on the Status bar and select it from the customize options.

7.5 Links

There are a number of options available to you if you want to create a link from one part of your document to another, or indeed link to another file or web address.

Bookmarks

Bookmarks allow you to specify a position within a document that can be returned to quickly from any other place in the file. A bookmark is inserted to set the position.

To insert a bookmark:

1 Place the insertion point or select the text or item to set the position for the bookmark.

2 Display the **Insert** tab.

3 Click **Bookmark** in the **Links** group.

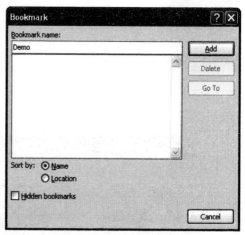

4 Give your bookmark a name.

5 Click **Add**.

To jump to the bookmark:

1 Click the **Bookmark** button on the **Insert** tab.

2 Select a bookmark from the **Bookmark name:** list.

3 Click **Go To**.

4 Close the **Bookmark** dialog box.

To delete a bookmark:

1 Click **Bookmark** on the **Insert** tab.

2 Select the **Bookmark** from the **Bookmark name:** list.

3 Click **Delete**.

4 Close the **Bookmark** dialog box.

Cross-reference

A cross-reference can be used to link to a range of objects within a file. You can link to numbered items, headings, bookmarks, footnotes, endnotes, equations, figures and tables. In a document, a cross-reference might appear as 'See Appendix 2' or 'See Table 3 above'. They are particularly useful for long documents that will be read on screen, where the reader can use the cross-reference to jump to other areas in the document (by default, cross-references are inserted as hyperlinks).

♦ You cannot create cross-references to an object in another document.

To insert a cross-reference:

1 Type in the text to introduce the cross-reference e.g. 'For more information, see...'

2 Click **Cross-reference** in the **Links** group on the **Insert** tab.

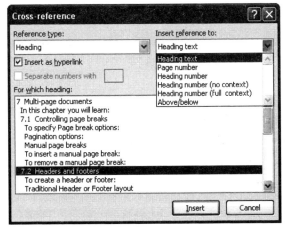

3 Select the **Reference type** from the list.

4 Choose an **Insert reference to:** option.

5 Leave the **Insert as hyperlink:** checkbox selected.

6 Select the item to cross-reference to from the list.

7 Click **Insert**.

8 Close the **Cross-reference** dialog box.

• To jump to a cross-reference in your document, hold down [**Ctrl**] and click on the cross-reference.

Hyperlink

A hyperlink can be used to create a link to an existing file or a web page, a place in the current document e.g. a bookmark, or create a link to a new document or to an e-mail address.

To insert a hyperlink to an existing file or a web page:

1 Position the insertion point where you want the hyperlink.

Or

2 Select the text you want to create a hyperlink from.

3 Click the **Hyperlink** button in the **Links** group.

4 Choose **Existing File or Web Page** in the **Link to:** panel.

5 Locate the file or type in the web address you want to link to.

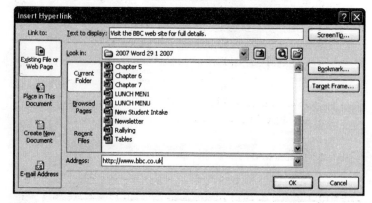

Other Link to: options

Place in This Document – displays reference points, e.g. headings, bookmarks, that you can link to.

Create New document – allows you to specify a location and name for your new document.

E-mail address – requests address information, and launches a New Message dialog box when clicked.

7.6 Document Map

Provided you have been using Heading styles to format the headings in your document and give it some structure, you can use the Document Map to quickly check the overall structure of your file and move around it quickly.

To work with the Document map:

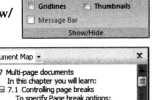

1   Select **Document Map** in the **Show/ Hide** group on the **View** tab.

◆   The map will open to the left of your document. You can resize the map by dragging its right-most border.

2   To move your insertion point to a heading displayed on the map, click on the heading.

3   To collapse and expand the document outline click the ⊞ (expand) and ⊟ (collapse) buttons.

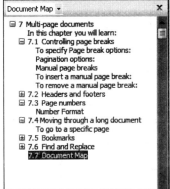

4   To close the map, deselect the **Document Map** checkbox, or click the **Close** button at the top right of the map.

Thumbnail view

This view may also be useful when working in a long document. The pages in the document are displayed in miniature in a pane on the left of the screen and you can jump to any page by clicking on its thumbnail.

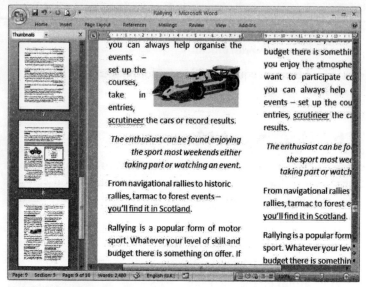

To switch Thumbnail view on/off:

♦ Select or deselect the **Thumbnails** checkbox in the **Show/Hide** group on the **View** tab.

7.7 Comments

Comments are useful if you want to add a note to some text in your document. The comments are a bit like 'Post-its', and can be used for suggestions, reminders or prompts.

To insert a comment:

1 Place the insertion point where you want to add a comment.

2 Click **New Comment** in the **Comments** group on the **Review** tab.

3 Enter your comment into the balloon.

4 Press **[Esc]** or click anywhere in your document to continue.

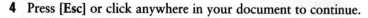

* Comments are displayed in a balloon on the right of the page.

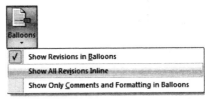

* Their appearance is controlled using the Balloons options.

If you turn on **Show All Revisions Inline**, the comment is reduced to a marker, and will be displayed if you put the mouse pointer over it.

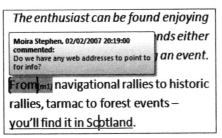

To edit a comment:

1 Show the balloons (if necessary).

2 Click inside the comment box and edit as normal.

Or

1 Click the **Reviewing Pane** button in the **Tracking** group (or click the arrow and choose the position of the reviewing pane).

2 Edit the comment in the reviewing pane.

3 Click the **Reviewing Pane** button again to close it.

To move through the comments:

* Click the **Next** and **Previous** buttons in the **Comments** group.

To delete a comment:

♦ Select the comment and click **Delete** in the **Comments** group.

To delete all comments:

♦ Click the arrow at the **Delete** button, and choose **Delete All Comments in Document**.

7.8 Track Changes

When editing a document you can switch the Track Changes option on. This allows you to mark the insertions and deletions that you are suggesting, and then you can do a separate sweep to decide whether or not you actually want the changes accepted. You can use this feature on your own documents, but it can be particularly useful when you are proofing one for someone else. You can make your suggestions, return the document to the author, then they can decide whether or not to accept your ideas.

To switch Track Changes on and off:

♦ Click **Track Changes** in the **Tracking** command group.

Work through the document, inserting and deleting as usual. Edits are displayed in a red font – the insertions are underlined and the deletions are marked with a line through them. A vertical line also appears at the left of the line that has been edited.

> Whatever your skill level of skill and budget there is something on offer.

The Balloon options will affect the way that the changes are displayed. You can also see the changes summarized in the Reviewing Pane if you display it.

You can change the options used when tracking changes.

1   Click the arrow under the **Track Changes** button then click **Change Tracking Options...**

2   Complete the dialog box as required.

3   Click **OK**.

What do you want to track, and how do you want to mark it up?

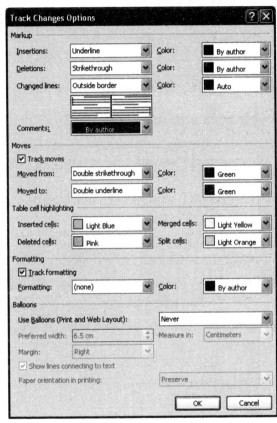

- If several people are working on a document, you can change the user name so that you know who has suggested what. Choose **Change User name...** from the **Track Changes** list.

Accept/Reject changes:

1   Click the **Next** and **Previous** buttons in the **Changes** group to move from one change to another.

2   To accept a change, click **Accept**.

Or

- Click the drop-down arrow and select an **Accept** option.

3 To reject a change, click **Reject**.

Or

- Click the drop-down arrow and select a Reject option.

7.9 Reference marks

Footnotes and endnotes

These are often used in longer documents to explain something in the main text – you will have seen them in books or reports. A footnote can be displayed below the text or at the bottom of the page. An endnote can be at the end of the section or document.

To create a footnote:

1 Place the insertion point where you want the footnote marker to appear.

2 Click **Insert Footnote** in the **Footnotes** group on the **References** tab.

3 Enter your footnote text (the insertion point will have been moved to the footnote area at the bottom of the page).

4 Click anywhere inside the main document area.

- The footnote text will be displayed when you move your mouse pointer over it.

> Demo of footnote.
>
> Rallying[1]

To create an endnote:

1 Place the insertion point where you want the Endnote marker.

2 Click **Insert Endnote** in the **Footnotes** group.

3 Enter your endnote text (the insertion point will have been moved to the endnote area at the end of the document).

4 Click anywhere inside the main document area.

To edit a footnote or endnote:

1 Double-click the footnote/endnote marker to take you to the text at the bottom of page/end of document.

2 Edit the text as required.

3 Click in the document area.

To delete a footnote or endnote:

• Delete the footnote or endnote marker in the document text. The numbering will be adjusted automatically.

To change a footnote to an endnote/endnote to a footnote:

1 Select the footnote/endnote (number and text).

Footnote and Endnote [?] [X]

Location
◉ Footnotes: Bottom of page ▼
○ Endnotes: End of document ▼
            Convert...

Format
Number format: 1, 2, 3, ... ▼
Custom mark: [   ]   Symbol...
Start at: 1 ⬍
Numbering: Continuous ▼

Apply changes
Apply changes to: Whole document ▼

[Insert]   [Cancel]   [Apply]

2 Right-click on the selected text.

3 Left-click on **Convert to Endnote/Convert to Footnote**.

To edit the settings:

1 Click the **Footnote and Endnote** dialog box launcher button at the bottom of the **Footnotes** group.

2 Select the options in the dialog box.

3 Click **OK**.

Captions

A caption is another type of reference mark often used in longer documents. They can be added to tables, graphs, etc. and are displayed above or below the object.

To add a caption:

1 Select the object.

2 Click **Insert Caption** in the **Captions** group on the **References** tab.

3 Edit the **Label, Position,** etc. as required

4 Click **OK**.

To edit a caption:

♦ Click within it and insert or delete text.

To remove a caption:

♦ Select it and press [**Delete**].

Caption

Caption:
FIGURE 1PROCEDURE FLOWCHART

Options

Label: Figure

Position: Below selected item

☐ Exclude label from caption

[New Label...] [Delete Label] [Numbering...]

[AutoCaption...] [OK] [Cancel]

AutoCaptions

If you want to add captions automatically when objects are inserted, you can use the AutoCaption feature.

1 Click **AutoCaption...** in the **Caption** dialog box.

2 Select the type of object to add captions to.

3 Specify the options and click **OK**.

Each time you add a new object of the type specified a caption will be added.

7.10   Outline view

If you create long, structured documents, e.g. reports, minutes or theses, Outline view is worth exploring. It gives an overview of the structure of a document by displaying main headings, subheadings, etc. Heading 1 is the highest level of heading, Heading 9 is the lowest. For most documents you'll probably use no more than four heading levels. Change to Outline view when you want to view or edit the structure of your file.

To go into Outline view:

♦ Click the **Outline** button on the Status bar.

Or

♦ Click the **Outline** button in the **Document Views** group on the **View** tab.

Structuring your file

If you enter your text in Print Layout view (which is probably the case), your file is structured as you apply the Heading 1 – Heading 9 styles to your headings and sub-headings.

If you enter text or adjust the structure in Outline view, use the command buttons in the Outline group to structure your text.

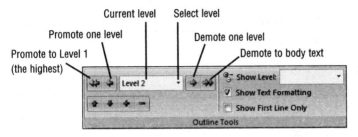

To set a heading level:

• Select the text and use the Level buttons to specify the level.

• You also change the level of a heading by clicking the drop-down arrow and selecting the level from the list.

Collapse and Expand

You can collapse or expand documents in Outline view to show the level of detail required. For example, you might want to view only the Heading 1 and Heading 2 levels within your file.

To collapse the whole document to a given level:

• Select the level from the Show Level: list.

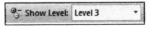

To expand the whole document again:

• Select **Show All Levels** from the list.

To collapse or expand individual areas in your document:

1 Place the insertion point inside the heading of the area that you want to collapse or expand.

2 Double-click the **Expand/Collapse** ⊕ button as required.

Or

♦ Click the **Expand** or **Collapse** tool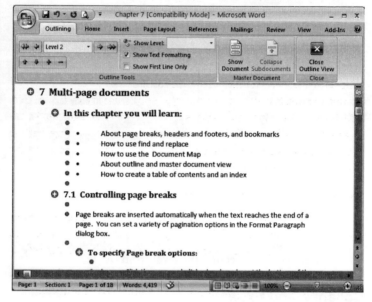

♦ You can also control the amount of body text displayed when the outline is expanded using the **Show First Line Only** checkbox.

Rearranging the structure

Outline view is great for letting you see the overall structure of your file. You can check that your headings are all in the right order and at the correct level. If you notice that you have a heading (and its substructure) in the wrong place, you can move it easily. You could cut and paste it, but there is in easier way in Outline view.

To rearrange the structure:

1 Expand or collapse your file until you can see the heading you want to move (if you want to move its substructure too, collapse it, so you can just see the heading).

2 Select the heading – place the insertion point within it.

3 Click the **Move Up** or **Move Down** buttons ⬆ ⬇ until the paragraph is in its new position.

♦ Any substructure the heading has will be moved with it.

Outline levels

The Word styles Heading 1 to Heading 9 are initially assigned to outline levels 1–9. You can assign your own styles to the outline levels. One way to do this is to base your styles on the headings – they will automatically pick up the corresponding outline level when you do this. You can also format styles to pick up the required outline level using the Paragraph dialog box.

To assign your own styles to the levels:

1 Modify the style you want to assign an outline level to. Right-click on it in the Quick Styles gallery or click the arrow to the right of the style in the task pane, and choose **Modify...**

2 In the **Modify Style** dialog box, click the **Format** button at the bottom left of the dialog box and choose **Paragraph...**

3 Select the **Indents and Spacing** tab.

4 Set the level required in the **Outline level** field.

5 Click **OK**.

7.11 Master document

A master document is a container for other documents. It is useful for very long documents, e.g. manuals or books, where you may have several files (perhaps one for each section or chapter). By collecting the files together into a master document, page numbering, headers and footers, table of contents and indexes can be generated more easily across all the subdocuments, as you have quick and easy access to each one without having to open and close individual files.

You can create subdocuments from within the master document or insert existing documents into a master document.

• Go into Outline view to work with a master document. Click **Show Document** in the **Master Document** group to display the Master Document buttons.

To create your subdocuments within your master document:

1 Create a new file – this will be your master document.

2 Type up your document – it may just be chapter headings/ section headings at this stage.

3 Format the headings that indicate where you want a new file created using the Heading styles (ensure that you use the same style for start-of-file heading).

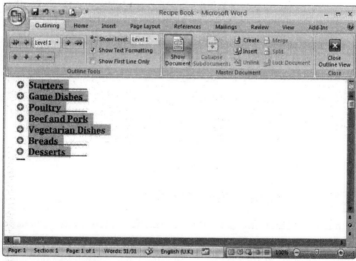

4 Save the master document file.

5 Go into Outline view.

6 Check and fix your file structure as necessary.

7 Select the headings and text to split into subdocuments.

8 Click the **Create** button in the **Master Document** group.

9 Save your master file again.

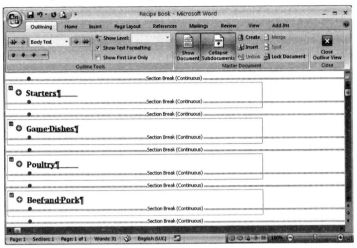

◆ Word will automatically save each subdocument, with the subdocument's heading used for the filename.

◆ Word inserts a continuous section break above and below each subdocument when you create them in this way.

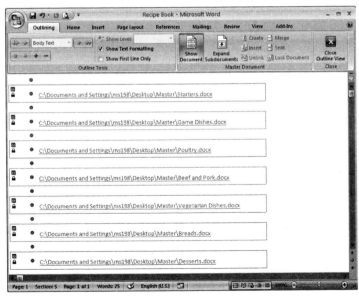

To insert an existing document into your master document:

1 Display your master document in Outline view.

2 If necessary, expand the master document – it must be expanded if you want to insert anything into it.

3 Place the insertion point where you want the subdocument.

4 Click **Insert** in the **Master Document** group.

5 Locate the file you want to insert.

6 Click **Open**.

♦ Word inserts a next page section break above and a continuous section break below the inserted document.

To open a subdocument from the master document:

♦ If the subdocuments are collapsed, press [Ctrl] and click on its name, or double-click on the icon beside the heading.

♦ If the subdocuments are expanded, double-click on the subdocument icon to the left of the subdocument heading.

When the subdocuments are expanded, you can use the Outline tools to control the detail displayed in your master document.

Unlink subdocument

You can also remove the link to a subdocument. When you unlink one, its text is converted to normal text in the master document.

To unlink a subdocument:

1 Expand the subdocuments.

2 Select the subdocument you want to break the link to.

3 Click the **Unlink** button to break the link between the master document and the subdocument.

Splitting and merging a subdocument

As a document develops, you might decide that a subdocument should be split up further, or several should be merged into one.

To split a subdocument:

1 Expand your subdocuments.

2 Enter a heading at the correct level, e.g. Heading 1, at each point you want the document split.

3 Select the original subdocument.

4 Click the **Split** button.

5 Save the master document.

To merge a number of subdocuments into one:

1 Expand the subdocument.

2 If necessary, move the subdocuments you wish to merge so that they are next to each other.

3 Select the documents – click the subdocument icon to the left of the heading of the first one, then hold [**Shift**] down and click the heading icon to the left of the last you want to merge.

4 Click the **Merge** button.

5 Save the master document.

Lock/Unlock subdocuments

All subdocuments are automatically locked when a master document is collapsed. Locked documents cannot be edited from the master document (but they can be opened from it, edited and saved as usual).

When expanded, subdocuments are automatically unlocked and can then can be edited from the master document.

To lock/unlock subdocuments that are expanded:

1 Select the document you wish to lock/unlock.

2 Click the **Lock Document** button.

If you lock a document that is expanded in the master document, you cannot edit it – it opens as a read-only file.

Unlock the subdocument again if you wish to edit it.

To print your master document:

1 Expand the subdocuments in Master Document view.

2 Go into Preview then print as usual.

7.12 Table of contents

You can quickly create a table of contents (TOC) for any document, if you have used the built-in heading styles to format the headings (see Chapter 5) or you have assigned outline levels to the styles that you have used for headings (see section 7.10).

To insert a table of contents:

1 Position the insertion point where you want the table of contents – usually at the beginning of the document.

2 Click **Table of Contents** in the **Table of Contents** group on the **References** tab.

3 Click a Built-in style.

Or

* Click **Insert Table of Contents...** near the bottom of the list.

4 Specify the options for your table of contents in the dialog box, e.g. number of levels, style, leader character, etc.

5 Click **OK**.

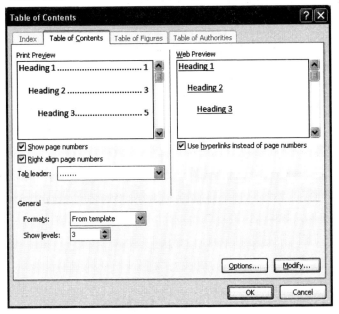

- If you want to specify styles other than Heading styles to be used to generate your table of contents, click **Options...** and select the ones you want from the dialog box.

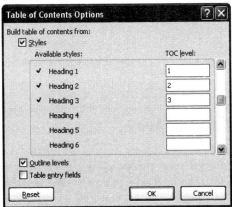

* To edit the formatting of the TOC entry, click the **Modify...** button and modify the formatting of the TOC styles.

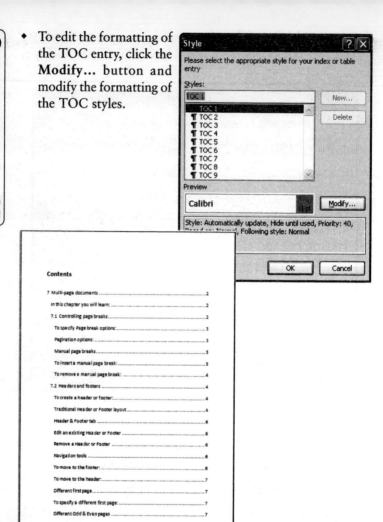

Using TC field codes

You can get Word to generate a TOC automatically, even if you haven't formatted your entries using the Heading styles. If you enter TC field codes into a document to indicate where the TOC entries are to be taken from, you can generate a table of contents using these codes rather than the heading styles.

To insert a TC field code:

1 Position the insertion point immediately in front of the text you are generating a TC code for.

2 Click **Quick Parts** in the **Text** group on the **Insert** tab.

3 Choose **Field...**

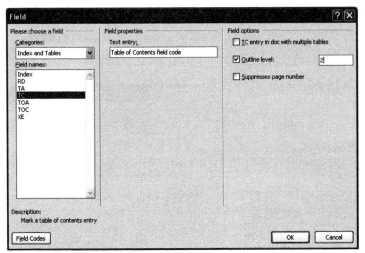

4 Select **Index and Tables** in the **Categories** list.

5 Select **TC** in the **Field names** list.

6 Type the text you want to appear in the table of contents in the **Text entry** area.

7 Set the options as required and click **OK**.

• TC field codes are normally hidden – click the **Show/Hide** button in the **Paragraph** group to display them.

{·TC··"Table·of·Contents·field·code"·\l·2·}¶

To generate a table of contents using field codes:

1 Place the insertion point where you want the TOC.

2 Click **Table of Contents** in the **Table of Contents** group on the **References** tab.

3 Click **Insert Table of Contents...** near the bottom of the list.

4 Click **Options...**

5 If you are not using Headings, deselect the **Styles** checkbox.

6 Select the **Table entry fields** checkbox.

7 Click **OK** then **OK** again to close the dialog box.

To get to a page quickly from your table of contents entry:

◆ Hold down [Ctrl] and click on the TOC entry.

To update the ToC:

1 Right-click on it, then click **Update Field**.

2 Select an update option and click **OK**.

7.13 Index

If your document needs an index, you can get Word to automate this process too. There are two steps to generating an index:

◆ Marking the entries you want to appear in the index.

◆ Creating the index.

To mark an index entry:

1 Select the word(s) you want to appear in your index.

2 Click **Mark Entry** in the **Index** group on the **References** tab.

3 The **Main entry:** field will display the selected text – edit it if necessary.

4 Click **Mark,** or **Mark All** to index all occurrences of the text.

5 The **Mark Index Entry** dialog box remains open so you can work through the document marking multiple entries.

6 Click **Close** when you've finished.

• If you later decide that you don't want a marked item indexed, click **Show/Hide** in the **Paragraph** group to show the index field codes, then delete any you don't want.

To create the index:

1 Place the insertion point where you want the index to appear – usually at the end of your file.

2 Click **Insert Index** in the **Index** group on the **References** tab.

3 Specify any options for your index and click **OK.**

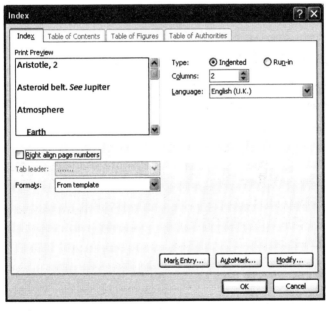

To update the index:

• Click the **Update Index** button in the **Index** group.

Updating will correct any page numbers that may have changed as a result of your document being edited.

Summary

This chapter has introduced many of the features that are particularly useful when working with long documents. We have discussed:

• Automatic and manual page breaks

• Headers and footers

• Page numbering

• Moving through multi-page documents

• Links – bookmarks, cross-references and hyperlinks

• The Document Map

• Comments

• Tracking changes

• Footnotes, endnotes and captions

• Using Outline view

• Master documents

• Creating a table of contents

• Creating an index.

08 templates and building blocks

In this chapter you will learn:

- how to use the standard templates
- about customizing templates
- how to create templates
- about controls
- how to protect templates
- about building blocks

8.1 Word templates

To create a document using the Blank Document template, you choose Blank Document from the New Document dialog box. The document is A4, portrait, with the margins set at 2.54 cm.

Word comes with several other templates. Look through these as you may find some of them useful. There are several letter, report, fax and résumé (CV) templates to choose from, as well as a blog.

If you find a template you would like to use, you can customize it with your own company details, etc. and save it for future use.

To create a document using a Word template:

1 Display the **New Document** dialog box.

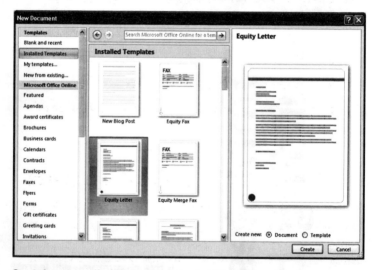

2 Select **Installed Templates** in the **Templates** list.

3 Scroll through the templates and select the one you want.

4 Click **Create**.

Explore the document that you have created. Check out the layout – notice that some templates include areas for your company name, address, telephone/fax, etc.

Many of the documents created using a Word template include details on how to use and complete the document. In the main, you just follow the instructions on the screen.

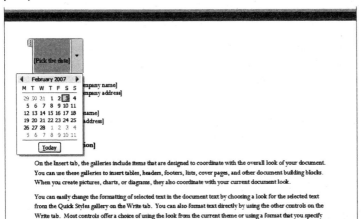

On the Insert tab, the galleries include items that are designed to coordinate with the overall look of your document. You can use these galleries to insert tables, headers, footers, lists, cover pages, and other document building blocks. When you create pictures, charts, or diagrams, they also coordinate with your current document look.

You can easily change the formatting of selected text in the document text by choosing a look for the selected text from the Quick Styles gallery on the Write tab. You can also format text directly by using the other controls on the Write tab. Most controls offer a choice of using the look from the current theme or using a format that you specify

To complete the document:

1 Click in the content holders and enter your text.

2 Delete any content holders you don't require.

3 Select and delete the sample text, and type in your own.

4 Save and print.

8.2 Customizing the Word templates

If you find a template that you like, but it isn't exactly what you want, you can customize it – perhaps by adding your company details, name, address, etc. – and save it as a template. It will then be just as you really want it to base new documents on.

You can customize any part of a template – page layout, headers, footers, styles, etc.

To customize your template:

1 Display the **New Document** dialog box.

2 Choose the template you wish to customize.

3 Select the *Template* option in the **Create new:** area.

4 Click **Create**.

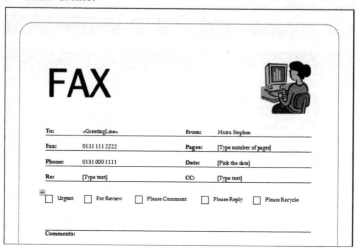

5 Edit the template as required.

6 Save your file – it should go into the *Templates* folder.

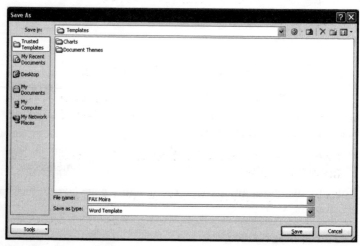

7 Close your file.

To create a document from your customized template:

1 Display the **New Document** dialog box.

2 Select **My Templates** in the **Categories**. Your template should be on the **My Templates** tab.

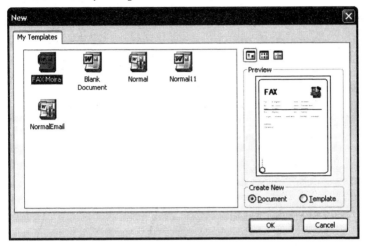

3 Select *Document* in the **Create New** options.

4 Click **OK**.

8.3 Creating your own template

You can easily create your own templates for the letters, reports and forms that you use. You can start with the Blank Document template, or any other template.

1 Create a new document based on an existing template, e.g. Blank Document.

2 Set up the standard text and layout for your template.

3 Save your file as a template – select *Word Template* in the **Save as type** field.

4 Close your file.

8.4 Controls

To make your template easier to use, you can add special fields
to it called Controls. These are mainly used for collecting data
on web forms. You will find them on the Developer tab.

To display the Developer tab:

1 Click the Microsoft Office button and choose **Word Options**.

2 In the **Popular** set, tick **Show Developer tab in the Ribbon**.

3 Click **OK**.

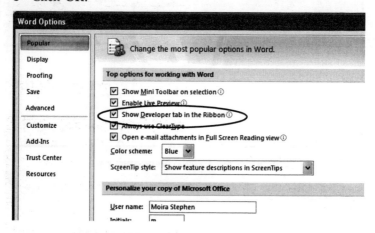

Four of the most useful controls are:

Date Picker – allows a user to select a date from a calendar.
This can be set to display the date in your preferred format.

Rich Text entry – can be formatted by the user.

Plain Text entry – cannot be formatted by the user.

Drop-down List – use when there are a limited number of
acceptable entries. You must go into the Properties to specify
the items that will be displayed in the list (see page 162).

To add controls:

1 Display the **Open** dialog box.

2 Select **Trusted Templates** in the panel.

3 Open the template you want to edit.

4 Display the **Developer** tab in the Ribbon.

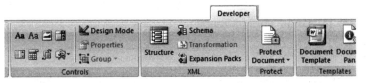

5 Position the insertion point where you want the control.

6 Click the control type in the **Controls** group.

7 Format the control – select it and click **Properties** in the Controls group.

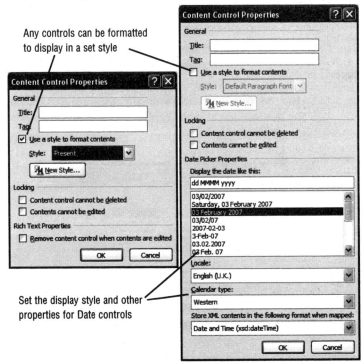

Any controls can be formatted to display in a set style

Set the display style and other properties for Date controls

To specify drop-down list properties:

1   Click **Add…** in the **Content Control Properties** dialog box.

2   Enter the **Display Name** of the item. This will be copied into the **Value** (the text to be shown in the list) – leave this.

3   Click **OK** to close the **Add Choice** dialog box.

4   Repeat steps 1–3 for each item.

5   If necessary, use the **Modify, Remove, Move Up** or **Move Down** buttons to get your list as you want it.

6   Click **OK**.

7   Save your template and close it.

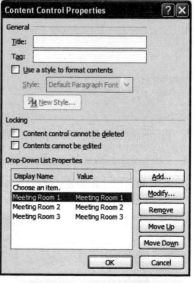

When you create a document based on your template, you will be able to use the controls to help you enter your information in the correct place and in the right format.

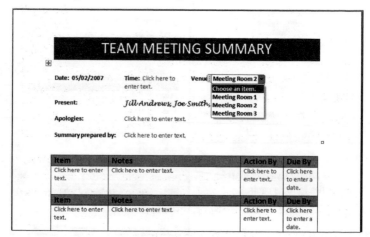

Templates and controls can be very useful when you want to ensure that documents of a particular kind maintain a consistent look.

To create a document from the template:

1 Start a new document based on the template.

2 Click on each control and enter the data required – with Date Picker and Drop-down list controls, select from the options.

3 Save, print or distribute as an e-mail attachment as usual.

8.5 Protect document

You can protect any document, but this feature is probably most used with forms. You will normally want to prevent anyone changing a form by accident, e.g. deleting controls, changing the standard text or layout, etc. To safeguard your form, you should protect it. This has the following effects:

• Data entry and edit is limited to controls – you can't change the template layout or standard information on it unless you unprotect your template again.

• If you protect it for filling in forms, users are restricted to completing the information required in the controls.

To protect your document:

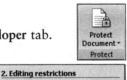

1 Click **Protect Document** on the **Developer** tab.

2 Select the **Editing Restrictions** checkbox on the **Restrict Formatting and Editing** panel.

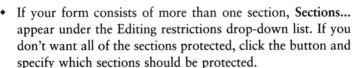

3 Choose *Filling in Forms* from the **Editing Restrictions** drop-down list.

• If your form consists of more than one section, **Sections...** appear under the Editing restrictions drop-down list. If you don't want all of the sections protected, click the button and specify which sections should be protected.

4 Click **Yes, Start Enforcing Protection**.

5 Enter your password.

6 Re-enter the pass-
word at the prompt.

7 Click **OK**.

8 Once you've com-
pleted your template,
save it and close it.

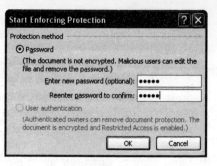

To edit the document, you will have to unprotect it. You will be
asked for the password when you try to unprotect it.

To unprotect your document:

1 Click the **Protect Document** button.

2 At the bottom of the **Restrict Formatting and Editing** panel,
click **Stop Protection**.

3 Enter your password.

4 Click **OK**.

Careful with passwords

**DO NOT forget your passwords. There is no magical way of
un-protecting a form if you don't know the password!**

**Passwords are case-sensitive – you must enter the same
pattern of upper and lower case characters each time.**

8.6 Completing a protected form

If a document is created from a protected form template, it can
be completed and printed this way.

1 Press [**Tab**] to move from one control to another, or click on
the control.

2 Complete the details as required.

3 Save the document.

Printing your form

To print onto plain paper:

Print in the normal way. The whole thing will print – standard text, borders, data in the form fields, etc.

To print onto pre-printed stationery:

1 Load the appropriate stationery into your printer.

2 At the **Print** dialog box, click **Options...**

3 Select the **Advanced** category.

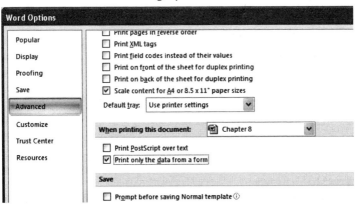

4 Scroll through to the **When printing this document:** options.

5 Select the **Print only the data from a form** checkbox.

6 Click **OK** to close the **Word Options** dialog box.

7 Click **OK** to print.

Building blocks

Building blocks, also called quick parts, are text, graphics or other document parts that you store and reuse. The building blocks are stored in galleries that can be accessed at any time. Building blocks can also be saved with templates and distributed with them – very handy for contract or letter templates that have standard content associated with them.

8.7 AutoText

Any text that you retype regularly, e.g. contract clauses, distribution lists, the standard opening or close to a general letter, can be stored as an AutoText entry. You can also store graphics in AutoText entries.

Once stored, an entry can be inserted into your documents with a few keystrokes or mouse clicks – even if it is several paragraphs long.

* Each AutoText entry must have a unique name.

To create an AutoText Entry:

1 Select the text you want to make into an AutoText entry. Include the paragraph mark at the end if you want the paragraph formatting saved with the entry.

2 Display the **Insert** tab.

3 Click **Quick parts** in the **Text** group and choose **Save Selection to Quick Part Gallery**.

Or

* Press [**Alt**]-[**F3**].

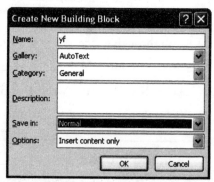

4 Accept the suggested name or edit it to suit.

5 Select the **Gallery** and **Category**.

6 Enter a description if you wish.

7 Specify the **Save in** location.

8 Select the **Options** required:

* **Insert content in its own page** – the building block is placed on a new page.

* **Insert in own paragraph** – content will not become part of

another paragraph, even if your cursor is in the middle of a paragraph.

• **Insert content only** for all other content.

9 Click **OK**.

To insert AutoText if you know the name of the entry:

1 Position the insertion point where you want the AutoText entry to appear.

2 Type in the AutoText entry name (don't put a space at the end of it).

3 Press [F3].

To find an AutoText entry:

1 Click **Quick Parts** in the Text group.

2 Select the entry from those displayed.

Or

3 Choose **Building Blocks Organizer...**

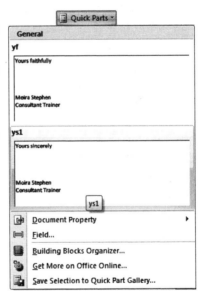

4 At the **Building Blocks Organizer** dialog box, click the column heading (Name, Gallery, Category, Template) to sort the list as required.

5 Locate and select the entry.

6 Click **Insert**.

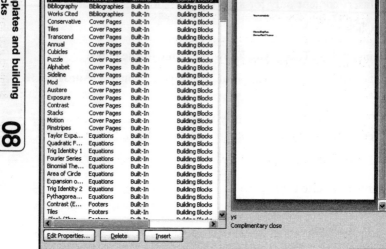

To delete an AutoText entry:

1 Click **Quick Parts** in the **Text** group and choose **Building Blocks Organizer...**

2 At the **Building Blocks Organizer** dialog box, click the column heading to sort the list as required.

3 Select the entry.

4 Click [Delete].

To edit the properties of an entry:

1 Open the **Building Blocks Organizer** dialog box and sort the list as required.

2 Select the entry.

3 Click **Edit Properties...**

4 Modify the entry as required.

5 Click **OK**.

6 Click **Yes** at the prompt to confirm the change.

7 Close the **Building Blocks Organizer** dialog box.

To replace the content of an AutoText entry:

1 Insert the entry into your document.

2 Amend the entry as necessary.

3 Select the entry again.

4 Press [**Alt**]-[**F3**].

5 Give the entry the same name and attributes as the original.

6 Click **Yes** at the prompt to confirm the change.

8.8 Cover pages

Another building block that can very quickly add the finishing touch and immediate impact to a document – especially a report – is a cover page. This is the front sheet for your document.

1 Position the insertion point at the beginning of the document.

2 Click **Cover Page** in the **Pages** group on the **Insert** tab.

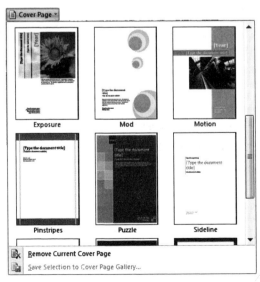

3 Select a page from those displayed.

4 Complete the page by adding detail to the content holders.

If you change you mind about your cover page, you can easily remove it.

To remove a cover page from your document:

1 Click **Cover Page** in the **Pages** group.

2 Select **Remove Current Cover Page**.

You can also design and save your own cover page so that you can reuse it on other documents.

To create your own cover page:

1 Create a cover page – use whatever fonts, borders, pictures, alignment options and content holders you require.

2 Select your page.

3 Click the **Cover Page** button.

4 Choose **Save selection to Content Page Gallery...**

5 Complete the dialog box as required.

6 Click **OK**.

Your page will be displayed in the General category of Cover Pages when you display the list (provided that is the category you chose).

You will also find it in the Building Blocks Organizer... dialog box (Text group, Quick Parts).

Quick Parts that can be accessed through other buttons include: equations, footers, headers, page numbers, table of contents, tables, text boxes and watermarks. Most of these have been or will be introduced in other chapters throughout the book.

Summary

In this chapter we have discussed:

* Using the templates that come with Word
* Customizing templates
* Creating templates of your own
* Adding controls
* Protecting your templates/forms
* Completing and printing a form
* Using AutoText entries to add standard text
* Cover pages.

09

mail merge

In this chapter you will learn:

- how to set up a main document
- how to create or open a data source document
- how to merge a data source
- how to sort and filter records
- about labels and envelopes

9.1 Mail merge terminology

Mail merge is used to produce customized standard letters, forms or mailing labels. It uses jargon and techniques similar to those found in database applications.

* **Main document** – the document that contains the layout, standard text and field names that point to the data source.

* **Data source** – the file containing the records for the mail merge, perhaps set of names and addresss. The data source is usually in a table layout, e.g. a Word file or an Access or Excel table. We will create ours in Word.

* **Record** – all the information on each item in your data source.

* **Field** – a piece of data in a record. Title, username, first name, telephone number, etc. would each be held in separate fields.

* **Field name** – the name used to identify a field.

* **Result document** – the one produced when you combine the records in the data source with the main document.

There are three steps involved in mail merge:

1 Creating the main document.

2 Creating and/or locating the data source.

3 Merging the two to produce the result document.

It doesn't matter whether you create the main document or data source first, but you must have both to get a result document.

If you are going to produce a mail merge letter, I suggest that you first type and save the standard letter. If you wish to use an existing file, open the one that will be your main document.

9.2 Basic mail merge

There are five steps to the process:

1 Create a mail merge main document.

2 Create or attach the data source file.

3 Add the merge field codes to the main document.

4 Preview the results.

5 Print or e-mail your documents.

The main document

The main document can be a letter, e-mail message, label, envelope or directory (list). We will set ours up as a letter. With letters, when you complete the merge, each record is merged into its own copy of the main document.

1 Type up your letter and save it, or open an existing letter.

2 Display the **Mailings** tab.

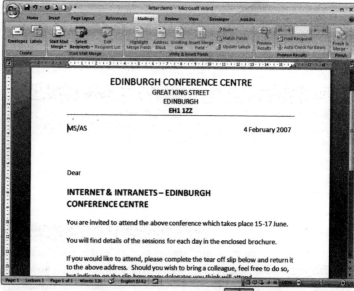

3 Click **Start Mail Merge** and choose Letters.

The data source

We will create a new data file in this example. If you have a data file that you want to use, you would select **Use Existing List...** and open the file. If you use Outlook you can **Select from Outlook Contacts...**

To create a new list:

1 Click **Select Recipients** on the **Mailing** tab.

2 Select **Type New List...**

3 At the **New Address List** dialog box, click **Customize Columns...**

4 At the **Customize Address List** dialog box, edit the field names as necessary. Add, remove or rename the fields, or move them into the order you want them.

5 Click **OK** to close the **Customize Address List** dialog box.

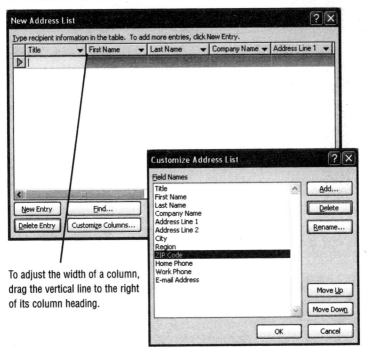

To adjust the width of a column, drag the vertical line to the right of its column heading.

Enter your names and addresses:

1 Type your data into the first column in the first row.

2 Press [Tab] to move to the next column.

3 Repeat 1 and 2 for each column, until the row is complete –
   leave empty any fields you don't have data for.

4 At the end of the first record, press [Tab] – a new entry will
   be created.

Or

♦ Click **New Entry**.

5 Repeat until all records have been entered.

6 Check your entries carefully, and amend any errors – click in
   the field and edit as necessary.

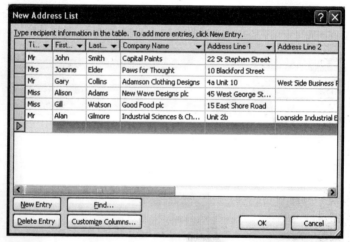

7 Click **OK**. The **Save Address List** dialog box is displayed.

8 Select the folder that you want to store the address list in –
   the default is *My Data Sources*.

9 Give your address list a name.

10 Click **Save**.

6

Issued

Branch: Lower Earley Library
Date: 23/08/2022   Time: 3:46 PM
ID: 2413000ᴢ214341

ITEM(S)   DUE DATE

Word 2007........................... 13 Sep 2022
34130001141364

Your current loan(s): 1
Your current reservation(s): 0
Your current active request(s): 0

If you would rather receive this
receipt by email please speak to a
member of staff.

*Please note - this receipt can be
recycled with your standard paper
recycling facilities.*

Thank you for using Wokingham
Libraries.

The merge fields

On saving the address list, you will be returned to the main document – the letter in this example.

To add merge fields:

1 Put the insertion point where you want the first merge field.

2 Click the arrow on **Insert Merge Field** on the **Mailing** tab.

3 Select the field you want to merge data from.

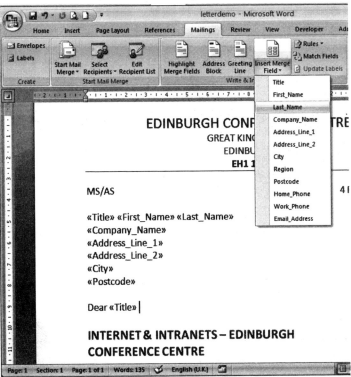

4 Repeat until all the fields required have been added.

• You can use the **Address Block** button to add the recipient's address, or the **Greeting Line** button to add the salutation.

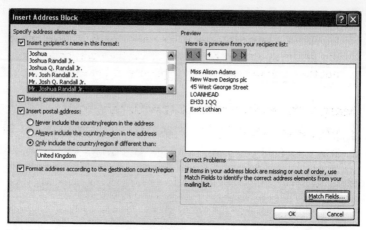

Insert Address Block dialog box – select or deselect the options to create the layout.

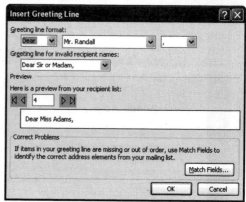

Insert Greeting Line dialog box – customize the format and line for invalid recipient names if necessary.

Preview Results

You should always preview your result document before you commit it to print.

To preview the result:

1 Click **Preview Results** in the **Preview Results** group.

2 The current record will be merged with the main document.

3 You can move through the records using the navigation buttons in the Preview Results group.

4 Click **Preview Results** again to cancel the preview.

• If you notice any problems in the preview, e.g. incorrect spacing or typing errors, fix the error on the main document – not the result document – then preview again to check it out.

Merge the main document with the data

1 Click the **Finish & Merge** button.

2 Select the merge option to use:

• **Edit Individual Documents...** if you want to create a result document that can be edited before printing.

• **Print Documents...** if you are sure that everything is OK.

• **Send E-mail Messages...** to e-mail the result document to the recipients.

3 In the **Merge to New Document** (or **to Printer** or **to E-Mail**) dialog box, choose **All,** or **Current record** or specify the range of records to be merged.

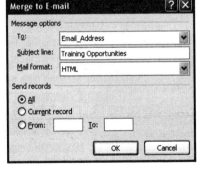

• In the **Merge to E-mail** dialog box, add a subject in the **Subject line.** The **Mail format** can be *HTML* (the default), *Attachment* or *Plain Text.*

4 Click **OK.**

The result document

If you merge to a new document you can make final adjustments to individual letters if you wish and check that the documents are satisfactory before you print.

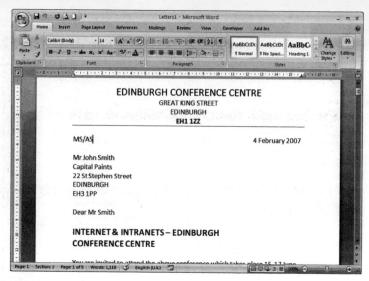

Things to note:

- The new file has a temporary filename, e.g. *Letters1*.

- There are many pages in it – to correspond with the number of records merged in and the length of the letter.

- Individual letters can be personalized if you wish.

- The file can be printed as normal.

- The result document is not usually saved. You can recreate it at any time from the main document and the data source.

9.3 Edit the data source

You can edit the data source by adding new records, deleting ones you no longer require or amending the contents of existing ones.

To edit the data source:

1 Click **Edit Recipient List** in the **Start Mail Merge** group.

2 Select the data source file in the **Data Source** list.

3 Click **Edit...** at the **Mail Merge Recipients** dialog box.

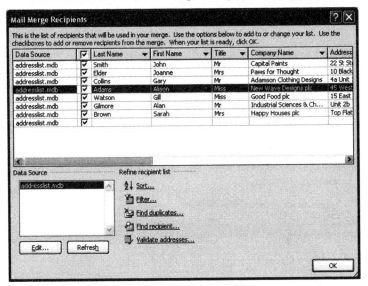

4 At the **Edit Data Source** dialog box, amend the data source as necessary.

• **To add a record,** click **New Entry** and enter the record.

• **To delete a record,** select the row then click **Delete Entry**.

• **To edit a record,** click in the field you wish to edit – this selects the field contents, and then:

  – Type to replace the current data.

  – Press [Delete] to delete the contents.

  – Click again to deselect the field, then insert and delete characters within it as required.

5 Click **OK** once all changes have been made in the **Mail Merge Recipients dialog box.**

6 At the prompt, click **Yes** to update the list and save the changes.

7 Click **OK** at the **Mail Merge Recipients** dialog box.

9.4 Sort

The records in your data source file are listed in the order that you typed them in. You can easily sort them into ascending order on any field, or indeed on several fields.

Simple sort

Use this method to sort your record on one field.

1 Click **Edit Recipient List** in the **Start Mail Merge** group.

2 Click the drop-down arrow to the right of the field name you want to sort on.

3 Select **Sort Ascending** or **Sort Descending** from the list.

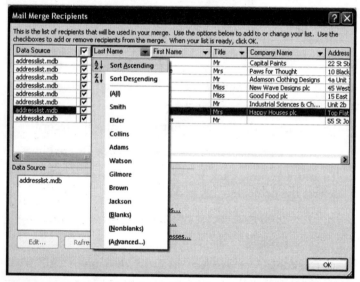

Multi-level sort

To sort your records on more than one field, e.g. by town, then by surname, use this method. You can sort on up to three fields.

1 Click **Edit Recipient List** in the **Start Mail Merge** group.

2 Under the **Refine recipient list** heading, click **Sort...**

3 On the **Sort Records** tab, click the drop-down arrow at the right of **Sort by:** and choose the main sort field from the list.

4 Set the sort order – **Ascending** or **Descending**.

5 Repeat steps 3 and 4 for the second-level sort field (and third level if necessary) in the **Then by:** fields.

6 Click **OK**.

9.5 Select recipients

By default, all the entries in your data source file will be merged with the main document. You can specify 'current record' and a range of consecutive records using the **From** and **To** fields when you complete your merge but this is limited in what it can achieve. A more flexible way of selecting recipients is to either select the recipients in the Mail Merge Recipients dialog box, or filter your data source file by specifying criteria.

To select records:

1 Click **Edit Recipient List** in the **Start Mail Merge** group.

2 Select or deselect the checkboxes to indicate which records you want merged.

3 Click **OK**.

◆ To select all records, select the checkbox in the header row.

◆ To deselect all records, clear the checkbox in the header row.

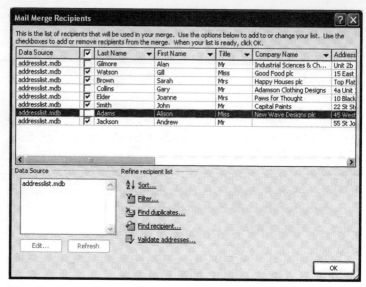

To select records according to specific criteria:

1 Click **Filter...** in the **Refine recipient list** area.

2 On the **Filter Records** tab, set the selection rules.

You can set up to six selection rules, joined by AND or OR.

* If all the selection rules must be met, link them with AND.

* If you want a record included using different selection rules, choose OR to separate each rule, or set of rules.

For example, to get records of recipients in Scotland or England, you need two selection rules linked by OR:

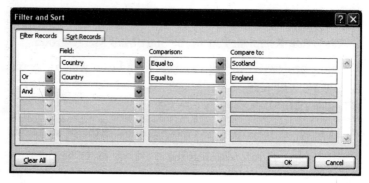

1 In the first, set the **Field** to *Country,* the **Comparison** to *Equal to,* and type 'Scotland' for the **Compare to** value.

2 Select OR as the joiner at the start of the second line.

3 Complete the second line as the first, but with 'England' for the **Compare to** value.

This dialog box shown next would select records that contain 'Scotland' in the Country field AND 'Perth' in the City field, OR 'England' in the Country field.

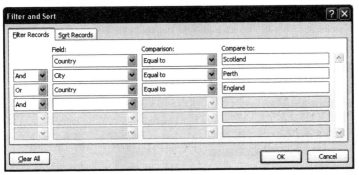

This last example will merge all records where the Country field contains 'Scotland' and also all records where the Country field contains 'England' except those records where the City field contains 'York'. Note the use of *Not equal to* as the **Comparison**.

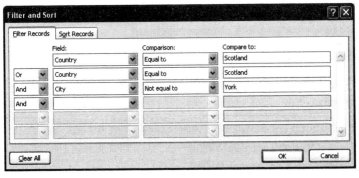

9.6 Mailing labels

You can merge your data source file with a range of different document types – letters (as above), labels, envelopes, etc.

Set up the labels

1 Create a new blank document.

2 Click **Start Mail Merge** and choose **Labels...** on the **Mailings** tab.

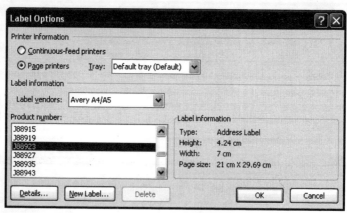

3 Edit the **Printer Information** if necessary.

4 Choose the **Label vendor** from the list.

5 Select the **Product number** required.

• If you want to add information on the label click **Details...**

• If you want to set up a custom label click **New Label...**

6 Click **OK**.

• A table is created, with columns and rows for each label.

Attach the data source

We will use the data source set up for the letter above.

1 Click **Select Recipients** in the **Start Mail Merge** group.

2 Select **Use Existing List...**

3 Open the data source file required.

Enter the merge fields

1 Enter merge fields onto the first label only.

«First_Name» «Last_Name»   «Next Record»

«Company_Name»

«Address_Line_1»

«Address_Line_2»

«City»

«Postcode»|

«Next Record»   «Next Record»

2 Once it is complete click **Update Labels** to replicate the fields in the other labels on the sheet.

«First_Name» «Last_Name»   «Next Record»«First_Name» «Last_Name»

«Company_Name»   «Company_Name»

«Address_Line_1»   «Address_Line_1»

«Address_Line_2»   «Address_Line_2»

«City»   «City»

«Postcode»   «Postcode»

«Next Record»«First_Name» «Last_Name»   «Next Record»«First_Name» «Last_Name»

«Company_Name»   «Company_Name»

«Address_Line_1»   «Address_Line_1»

«Address_Line_2»   «Address_Line_2»

«City»   «City»

«Postcode»   «Postcode»

Save your main document so that you can reuse the label format. In future you will just need to:

1 Open the main document file for your labels.

2 Attach the source data file, using **Select Recipients**.

3 Merge and print your labels (remember to load your labels into your printer!).

John Smith
Capital Paints
22 St Stephen Street
EDINBURGH
EH3 1PP

Joanne Elder
Paws for Thought
10 Blackford Street
EDINBURGH
EH10 2QQ

Alison Adams
New Wave Designs plc
45 West George Street
LOANHEAD
EH33 1QQ

Gill Watson
Good Food plc
15 East Shore Road
DALKEITH
EH44 1ZZ

9.7 Envelopes, e-mail and directories

Merging to envelopes or e-mail is very similar – just select the appropriate option at Start Mail Merge. (And remember to load the envelopes into your printer!)

You can add links to websites, or other areas in your e-mail to help direct the recipients to information.

Directories

A directory creates a list from your data source. I prefer to use a one row table to set up the main document, but you could use tabs if you prefer.

«First_Name» «Last_Name»	«Company_Name»	«Email_Address»	«Work_Phone»

When creating a directory, always choose **Edit individual documents** at the final stage. You can then finish off formatting your result document by adding a header row, etc.

Name	Company	E-mail	Work Number
John Smith	Capital Paints	johns@hotmail.com	0131 445 100
Joanne Elder	Paws for Thought	joannee@virgin.net	0131 555 1111
Gary Collins	Adamson Clothing Designs	garyc@blueyonder.co.uk	0131 666 2000
Alison Adams	New Wave Designs plc	adamsa@hotmail.com	0131 555 2020
Gill Watson	Good Food plc	gillwatson@yahoo.co.uk	0131 222 4888
Alan Gilmore	Industrial Sciences & Chemicals Ltd	alanindust@hotmail.com	0131 554 6622
Sarah Brown	Happy Houses plc	happyhouses@yahoo.co.uk	0131 227 3311
Andrew Jackson		ajackson@virgin.net	0131 444 3333

Summary

In this chapter we have discussed:

♦ Setting up the main document

♦ Creating and editing a data source file in Word

♦ Merging the main document and data source file to create a result document

♦ Editing the data source structure

♦ Sorting the records

♦ Selecting the records required by filtering

♦ Creating and printing mailing labels

♦ Envelopes, e-mail and directories.

10

illustrations

In this chapter you will learn:

- how to add pictures and clip art to your file
- about SmartArt objects
- how to add impact with WordArt
- how to draw with shapes
- how to build equations

10.1 Pictures

Most people have digital cameras, or access to the Internet and as a result of this often have many pictures stored on their computer. You can add pictures to your Word documents to make them more interesting or to illustrate a point.

To add a picture to your document:

1 Place the insertion point where you want the picture.

2 Click the **Picture** button in the **Illustrations** group on the **Insert** tab.

3 Locate the folder that contains your picture.

4 Select the picture and click **Insert**.

When you insert a picture, the Picture Tools are displayed on the Ribbon. You can use the tools to manipulate your pictures.

Basic picture handling skills

To delete the picture:

1 Click on it to select it.

2 Press [Delete].

To resize the picture:

• Drag one of the handles in a corner or along an edge.

You can also use the **Height and Width** fields in the Size group to specify an exact size for your picture.

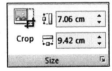

The Size dialog box offers more options for size and rotation.

1 Click the launcher at the bottom right of the **Size** group to open the dialog box.

2 Set the size options required on the **Size** tab.

3 Specify a rotation value if you wish.

4 Click **Close**.

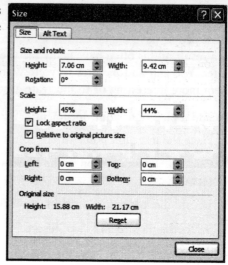

Formatting your picture

You can format a picture using the buttons on the **Format** tab of the Picture Tools.

Position

The **Position** button allows you to position your picture on the page, and also to choose a text wrapping option.

To position a picture:

1 Click on the **Position** button in the **Arrange** group.

2 Select the position relative to the text from the options.

♦ **More Layout Options...** opens the **Advanced Layout** dialog box where you can specify other options, e.g. the amount of space to leave between your picture and the surrounding text.

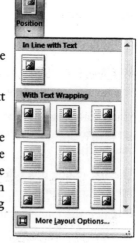

Text Wrapping

The **Text Wrapping** button also gives access to the various text wrapping options. If you set the option to *Square* (using the Advanced Layout dialog box or the Text Wrapping button) you can drag and drop your picture and position it anywhere within your text.

Crop

The Crop option in the Size group allows you to trim the edges off the picture.

To crop the picture:

1 Click the **Crop** button.

2 Drag a resize handle to crop the bits you don't want.

Or

1 Click the dialog box launcher at the bottom right of the **Size** group.

2 Set the **Crop from** options on the **Size** tab.

3 Click **Close**.

Adjust group

• **Brightness** – increase or decrease the brightness.

• **Contrast** – increase or decrease the contrast.

• **Recolor** – select from a variety of colour modes.

• **Compress Pictures** – reduces the size of the picture to give you a smaller file size.

• **Change Picture** – lets you change the picture, while preserving the formatting and size options set for the current one.

• **Reset Picture** – discards all formatting and resets the object to how it was when inserted.

- Apply a pre-set style from the **Picture Styles** list.

Or

- Use the **Picture Shape**, **Picture Border** and **Picture Effects** buttons to apply each formatting option individually.

10.2 Clip art

Office comes with hundreds of clip art images that can be added to your documents. You will also find many more clips on the Internet.

To add clip art to your document:

1 Position the insertion point where you want the clip art.

2 Click the **Clip Art** button in the **Illustration** group.

3 If you are looking for something specific, enter a keyword in the **Search for:** field.

4 Select your options in the **Search in:** and **Results should be:** fields.

5 Click **Go**.

6 Scroll through the pictures and select one.

The Picture Tools can be used to format your clip art in the same way as when working with your pictures.

10.3 SmartArt

There are about 80 different SmartArt objects you can choose from, to create all sorts of illustrations. List, process, cycle, hierarchy, relationship, matrix and pyramid are all represented. Browse through them to see what is on offer. You may find that not all options are available for all objects, but most will be.

Once you have chosen an object you can use the buttons on the **Design** tab to:

- Add shapes
- Promote and demote shapes
- Reverse the object
- Change the style
- Reset your graphic

- Enter and edit text
- Add bullets
- Select a layout
- Choose colours for a style

On the **Format** tab you can:

- Change your shapes
- Format individual elements

- Select a shape style
- Layer or rotate your shape

To create a SmartArt object:

1 Click the **SmartArt** button in the **Illustrations** group.

2 At the **Choose a SmartArt Graphic** dialog box, select a category from the list on the left.

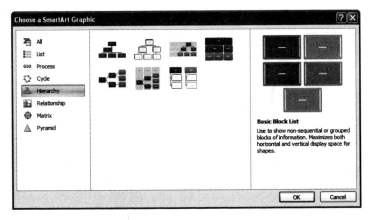

3 Select a style from the middle section. A preview and brief description will be displayed on the right.

4 Click **OK**.

Hierarchy

These charts are used for relationships that can be illustrated in a hierarchical way. Their most common use is probably to illustrate an organization chart. We will work through the options for creating an organization chart here, then you can adapt them as necessary as you work with other SmartArt graphics.

* Create your organization chart following **To create a SmartArt object:** above. The chart will be displayed on your page.

The SmartArt tools, with a Design and Format tab, are displayed when the organization chart is selected.

Entering text

You can enter text into your organization chart using the Text pane or you can type directly into the boxes on the chart.

* To open or close the Text pane, click the **Text Pane** button in the **Create Graphic** group.

To enter text using the Text pane:

1 Click at the bullet point by the item you want to add detail for.

2 Type in your text.

3 If you have more than one line of text to add at a point, press [Shift]-[Enter] to create new lines as necessary.

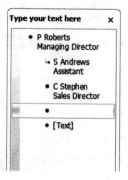

To enter text using a box:

1 Click in the box and type in your text.

2 If you have more than one line of text to add in the box, press **[Enter]** or **[Shift]-[Enter]** to create a new line.

◆ You can edit text directly into the box or using the Text pane. Click the arrows at the left of the chart to open the pane.

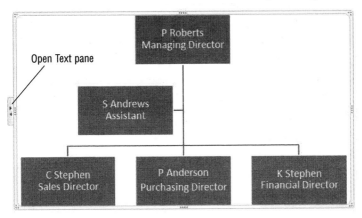

Adding and deleting shapes

You can build your chart up by adding shapes. Each new shape must be related to an existing one.

To add a shape:

1 Select the shape that you want to relate a new shape to.

2 Click the **Add Shape** tool in the **Create Graphic** group.

3 Select the option required from the list.

4 Enter your text.

To delete a shape:

1 Select the shape and press **[Delete]**.

2 If you change your mind, click **Undo** on the Quick Launch toolbar, or press **[Ctrl]-[Z]**.

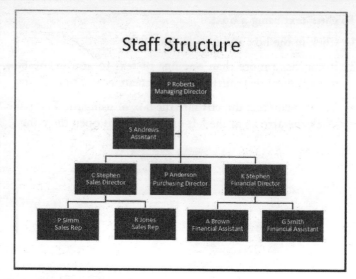

Organization chart layout

This option allows you to change the layout of a branch of your organization chart.

1 Select the parent shape (one that has other shapes below it).

2 Choose a format from the **Layout** options in the **Create Graphic** group.

Reverse graphic

◆ You can reverse the whole graphic, left to right, by clicking the `⇄ Right to Left` button in the **Create Graphic** group.

Promote and Demote

There may be times when you have a chart set up, then someone moves to a new job so their position within the hierarchy changes. You can promote or demote any shape using the **Promote** and **Demote** buttons in the Create Graphic group. This feature works best if you show the Text pane.

1 Select the point you wish to promote/demote.

2 Click the **Promote** or **Demote** button.

Layout

To change the overall layout used in your chart, select an option from the **Layout** group on the **Design** tab.

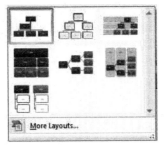

Style and colours

The options on the **SmartArt Styles** group provide a variety of styles and colours. There are simple styles, 3-D styles, and eight different colour themes, with several combinations within each.

Reset graphic

If you have been experimenting with the many options, you might finally decide to go back to the original formatting.

• To discard all your changes, click the **Reset Graphic** button in the Reset group.

Format tab

This tab offers more options. Experiment with them to see how they work. Many of the options here also apply to other shapes and WordArt objects.

The **Shapes** group can be used to change the shape of individual boxes in your diagram or make the shape larger or smaller.

The **Shape Styles** group lets you choose a standard style for your shape or specify the Fill, Outline and Effects options individually.

The **Size** group allows you to specify the exact height or width of the selected shape.

The **Arrange** group gives access to the Selection pane, and the options for setting the position of the shape in relation to other objects.

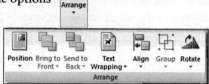

10.4 WordArt

WordArt lets you create special text effects. You can produce stunning title pages and real eyecatchers wherever needed.

1 Click the **WordArt** button in the **Text** group on the **Insert** tab.

2 Pick a style.

3 Type in your text.

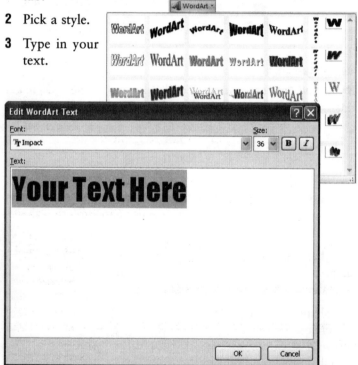

4 Select the **Font** and **Size**, and turn on **Bold** and/or **Italic** if required.

5 Click **OK**.

The WordArt tools are displayed when a WordArt object is selected.

Experiment with the various options to see what effect they have. To summarize:

Text group – The buttons in this group allow you to edit your text, change the text spacing, toggle between all characters being the same height and upper/lower case differentiation, change text direction, or set the alignment within the shape.

WordArt Styles – Choose a style, or format the fill, line and shape effects individually.

Shadow Effects – Add a shadow effect and nudge it in the direction required.

3-D Effects – Add and adjust 3-D effects.

Arrange – Adjust the position, text wrap, alignment and rotation options.

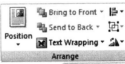

Size – Set a specific size for your WordArt object.

10.5 Shapes

You can use the Shapes command buttons to add different effects to your document, e.g. you could draw an arrow, with a message attached, pointing to a table or a picture on your page.

There are basic shapes, e.g. rectangles and ovals, block arrows, flowchart symbols, callouts and stars and banners. You can combine them to make diagrams and illustrations, or create something unique using the freehand drawing tools in the Lines group.

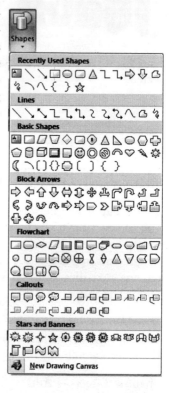

To draw a shape:

1 Click the **Shapes** button in the **Illustrations** group.

2 Select a shape.

3 Click and drag on your page to draw the shape.

♦ For a perfect square or circle, select the Rectangle or Oval shape, and hold down [**Shift**] as you click and drag.

Drawing Tools

When you select a drawing shape, the Drawing Tools appear in the Ribbon. If no shape is selected, they disappear again. You can use the buttons on the Format tab to format your shapes.

To format your shape in any way, you must select it first. Deselect it when you have finished.

To move or resize your shape:

- Click and drag within the object to move it.

- Click and drag a handle on a corner or edge to resize it.

If your shape must be a specific size, use the **Size** buttons in the Size group.

To delete a shape:

- Select it, then press [**Delete**].

Shape Styles

Use the Shape Styles buttons to select a different formatting style for your shape.

The options on the right are (top to bottom):

- **Shape Fill** gives access to all the fill options available for an object, e.g. colour, picture, gradient or texture.

- **Shape Outline** gives access to all the line formatting options for the shape outline, e.g. colour, weight, dashes and arrows.

- **Change shape** lets you change the shape, but keep all the formatting attributes that you have set.

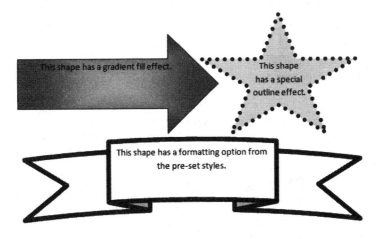

Adding text and text boxes

To add text to a shape:

1 Right-click on the shape.

2 Select **Add Text**.

3 Type your text into the shape.

If you wish to add free text to your document, (not within a shape or other object), you can use a text box. A text box can be positioned anywhere on your page.

To insert a text box:

1 Click the **Text Box** button in the **Recently Used Shapes** category, or the **Basic Shapes** category.

2 Drag to draw a rectangle where you want the text box to be.

3 Type in your text.

4 Click outside your text box.

Text commands

The text box can be resized, moved, formatted or deleted like any other shape. Several options that are specific to text boxes can be found in the **Text** group.

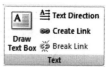

♦ Click the **Text Direction** button to change its direction.

Linking text boxes

If you want text to flow from one text box to another you can link them.

To link text boxes:

1 Select the text box that you want to create a link from.

2 Click the **Create Link** button.

♦ The pointer changes to a pitcher shape, so you can pour the text from one text box to another.

3 Click inside the text box that you want to create a link to.

Now is the time for all good men to come to the aid of the party. The quick brown fox jumped over the lazy	dog. To be or not to be, that is the question. Now is the time for all good men to come to the aid of	the party. To be or not to be that is the question. Now is

To break the link:

1 Click the **Break Link** button.

2 Click inside the text box that you linked from.

3-D effects and shadows

You can create some interesting effects with shapes, using the shadow, 3-D, layer and group options, or rotate or flip options.

3-D effects

There are a huge number of 3-D effects to choose from for your shape. Experiment with them to see what works best for you, and creates the effect you require.

To add a 3-D effect:

1 Click the **3-D Effects** button.

2 Select **3-D Effects,** then the effect that you want to use.

3 Use the tilt command buttons to adjust the amount of tilt on your 3-D shape.

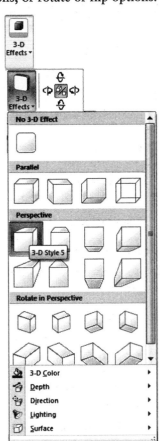

You can produce sophisticated results with the Depth, Direction, Lighting and Surface options.

Shadow effects

Use the Shadow Effects group to add shadows to your shapes. Once an effect has been added, you can control it using the buttons on the right. Use the nudge buttons to adjust the position of the shadow effect, and switch it on or off using the middle one.

10.6 Arranging shapes

Bring to Front, Send to Back

When you draw your shapes, they are placed in layers on your page. The first shape is on the lowest layer, the next one is on the one above, the third on another layer above that, and so on. If you move your shapes so that they overlap each other a little you will see this layering effect.

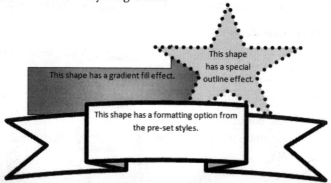

You can move a shape from one layer to another using the Bring Forward/ Send Backward commands. These are located in the Arrange group on the Format tab of the Drawing tools.

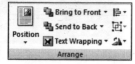

Bring to Front

*   **Bring to Front** moves the shape to the top of the pile.

- **Bring Forward** moves a shape forward one layer at a time.

- **Bring in Front of Text** places it on top of the document text.

Send to Back

- **Send to Back** moves the shape to the bottom of the pile.

- **Send Backwards** moves a shape back one layer at a time.

- **Send Behind Text** places the shape behind the document text.

Grouping

If you create an image from several shapes, you will find it easier to manage the final image if you group them together. Once the shapes are grouped they can be moved and resized as one object.

You can Ungroup the objects if you wish to edit individual shapes.

To group shapes:

1 Select the shapes – select the first shape, then hold down [**Shift**] and click on each of the other shapes.

2 Click the **Group** button in the **Arrange** group, then click

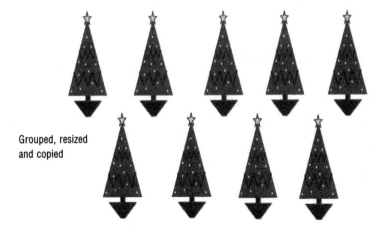

Grouped, resized
and copied

Group from the options displayed.

The shapes are grouped together into one object and can then be resized, moved or deleted as one. If you need to work on an individual shape again, you must ungroup the object again.

To ungroup your shapes:

1 Select the grouped shape.

2 Click the **Group** button.

3 Select **Ungroup** from the list.

♦ Edit the shapes as necessary.

To regroup the shapes that have been ungrouped:

1 Click the drop-down arrow to the right of the **Group** tool.

2 Choose **Regroup**.

Rotate and Flip

Shapes can be rotated left or right 90°, or freely through any angle, or flipped horizontally or vertically.

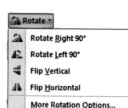

To rotate a shape:

1 Select the shape.

2 Choose an option from the **Rotate** button in the **Arrange** group.

10.7   Equations

If you use equations in your papers, you will find all the tools you need in the Equation feature in Word.

You can insert an equation by:

♦ Selecting the equation from a list of commonly-used ones.

♦ Typing or inserting the symbols.

♦ Inserting commonly-used math structures.

When working with an equation, the Equation Tools are displayed. Explore the options on the Design tab to see what is available.

To select an equation from a list of commonly used ones:

1 Click the arrow to the right of the **Equation** button in the **Symbols** group on the **Insert** tab.

Or

* Click the arrow under **Equation** in the **Tools** group of the **Equation Design** tab.

2 Select the equation from the list.

$$f(x) = a_0 + \sum_{n=1}^{\infty} \left(a_n \cos\frac{n\pi x}{L} + b_n \sin\frac{n\pi x}{L} \right)$$

To type the equation in, or insert symbols:

1 Click the **Equation** button.

2 Use the options in the **Symbols** group of the **Equation Design** tab, and/or your keyboard to enter the equation.

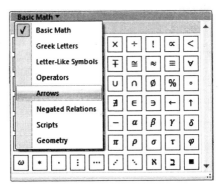

To insert your equation using math structures:

1 Select a structure from the **Structures** group on the **Equation Design** tab.

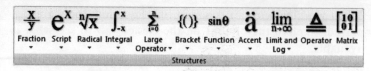

2 If the structure contains a placeholder, click in the placeholder and enter the symbol detail through the keyboard or from the Design tab.

Summary

This chapter has discussed the illustrations that can be created using a range of objects. We have looked at:

- Pictures
- Clip art
- SmartArt
- WordArt
- Shapes
- Equations.

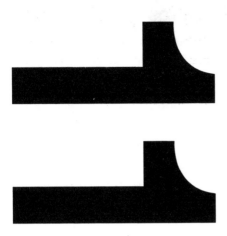

macros

In this chapter you will learn:

- about macros
- how to create, edit, run and delete macros
- how to assign macros to tools on the Quick Access toolbar

11.1 What are macros?

Macros can be used to automate a routine that you perform regularly. A macro is a set of Word commands grouped together so that you can execute them as a single action. If you perform a task often, but cannot find a keyboard shortcut or command button that runs through the sequence that you want to use, you should record the commands into a macro. You have then created a custom command.

What could you use a macro for?

* Setting up specific print instructions.

* Speeding up routine editing and formatting.

* Adding an equation to your file.

* Combining a group of commands that you often execute in the same sequence.

Two ways to create macros in Word:

* **Recording.** We will be using this option. You can record any feature that you can access through the Ribbon and dialog boxes.

* **Visual Basic Editor.** With this you can create powerful, flexible macros that can include Visual Basic as well as Word commands. We will take a brief excursion into the Editor when we discuss editing macros.

11.2 Recording a macro

Before you start recording your macro, think through what it is that you want to do. If there are any commands that you're not sure about, try them out first to check that they do what you want to include. For example, a macro to print the current page should record the steps:

1 Click the Microsoft Office button and open the **Print** dialog box.

2 Select *Current page* in the **Page Range** options.

3 Click **OK**.

Once you know what you need to record, you can create your macro. In the example below we will assign the macro to a tool on the Quick Access toolbar. You must have the Developer tab displayed.

To display the Developer tab:

1 Click the Microsoft Office button and go into **Word Options**.

2 Select **Show Developer Tab in the Ribbon** from the **Popular** category.

3 Click **OK**.

On the Developer tab, the Macro buttons are displayed in the Code group.

To start recording your macro:

1 Click the **Record Macro** button.

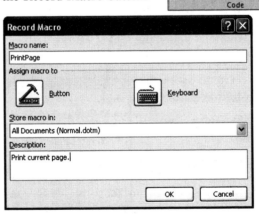

2 Enter a name (no spaces) for your macro in the **Macro name** field (don't use the default *Macro1, Macro2*, etc. – you'll never remember what you recorded in each one).

3 If you want your macro to be available in all documents, store it in the default *All Document (Normal.dotm)* file.

4 Enter a **Description**.

5 Click **OK**.

The Word Options dialog box will be displayed.

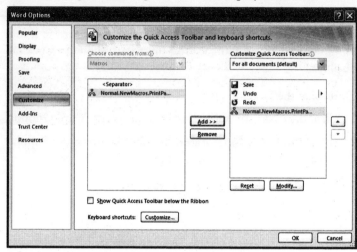

6 Add the macro to the Quick Access toolbar.

To change the standard text label to a graphic:

1 Click **Modify…** under the Quick Access toolbar list in the **Word Options** dialog box.

2 Select an icon from the **Modify Button** dialog box.

3 Edit the display name if you wish.

4 Click **OK** at the **Modify Button** dialog box.

5 Click **OK** at the **Word Options** dialog box.

You will be returned to your document.

To record your macro:

1 Perform the sequence of commands you want to record – if you are recording the steps to print the current page, click **OK** at the **Print** dialog box to send the page to the printer.

2 If you need to pause recording your macro (perhaps to check something) click the **Pause Record- ing** button. This then becomes **Resume Recorder** – click it when you're ready to restart recording.

3 Click **Stop Recording** when you've finished.

11.3 Play back your macro

This couldn't be easier!

♦ Click the new tool on the Quick Access toolbar.

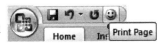

11.4 Delete a macro

If you record a macro and then decide that you don't want to keep it, you can delete it from the Macros area.

1 Click **Macros** in the **Code** group on the **Developer** tab.

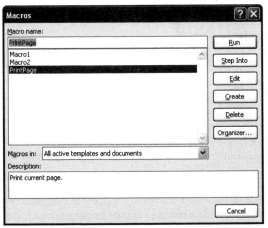

2 Select the macro from the list in the **Macros** dialog box.

3 Click **Delete**, then **Yes** at the prompt that asks if you're sure.

4 Close the **Macros** dialog box.

11.5 Edit a macro

With a short macro, it may be quicker to re-record it than to edit it in the Visual Basic editor. If you do decide to re-record one, and give it the same name as the original, Word will ask if you want to overwrite the original. Select **Yes** if you want to replace the original macro with the new one.

To make a minor adjustment to a larger macro, it is probably quicker to edit it in the Visual Basic Editor. When editing, be very careful not to delete anything that you don't understand, or insert anything that should not be there – you might find that it no longer runs properly if you do. If the worst comes to the worst and the macro stops working, you can always record again.

To edit a macro:

1 Click **Macros** in the **Code** group.

2 Select the macro from the list in the **Macros** dialog box.

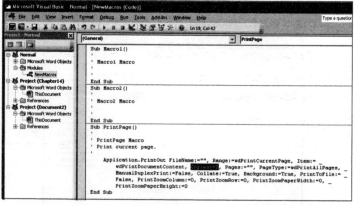

The Visual Basic code often has far more lines of code than commands you recorded. Don't worry about this – some instructions are picked up from default settings in dialog boxes. Scroll through until you recognize the part you want to change.

3 Click **Edit**.

4 Scroll through the code until you see the item you wish to edit.

5 Amend as necessary – I changed number of copies from 1 to 2 in this example.

6 Click the **Save Normal** tool on the toolbar.

7 Close the Visual Basic Editor – click the **Close** button or choose **Close and Return to Microsoft Word** from the File menu.

11.6 More ideas for macros

You could use macros to:

- Create a new document based on one of your own templates.
- Print and close the current file, and then create a new blank document.
- Apply a set of formatting options to your text.

Summary

In this chapter we have discussed:

- Recording a macro
- Assigning the macro to a Quick Access toolbar button
- Playing back a macro
- Deleting a macro
- Editing a macro.

12

Word and other applications

In this chapter you will learn:

- about linking and embedding
- how to use Word with Excel
- about charts
- how to create documents from PowerPoint slides
- about using Access data in a mail merge

12.1   Linking vs embedding

Word is part of Microsoft Office, and it integrates very well with the other applications in the suite. If you have installed the complete suite then you have the benefit of being able to use the best tool for each job. This chapter discusses some ways in which the Office applications can be integrated.

When you work through this chapter, you will come across the terms *linking* and *embedding*. Both these techniques enable you to incorporate data from other applications into your Word document. The main difference between linked data and embedded data lies in where it is stored and how it is updated.

Linked data

Linked data is not stored in your Word document. It is stored in the file, e.g. a workbook or presentation, which was created by the source application. When the data is updated within the source application the changes are reflected in the Word document to which it is linked.

Features of linking data include:

* The Word document is kept smaller.
* The data in the Word document is up to date.

Embedded data

Embedded data is stored in your Word document and does not exist as a separate file. However, when you create and edit the data, you have access to all the functions within the source application.

Features of embedded data:

* All the data is held in one document.
* When creating and editing the object you will have access to powerful features that are not part of the Word application.

The following sections discuss some of the methods you can use to integrate data across the applications in Office.

12.2   Copy and Paste

You can copy text, data, graphics, charts, etc. from one Office applicaton to anoher using simple copy and paste techniques.

To copy and paste between applications:

1   Launch Word and the application you want to copy from.

2   Select the object, text or data you want to copy.

3   Click the **Copy** button in the **Clipboard** group.

4   Switch to Word.

5   Place the insertion point where you want the data to appear.

6   Click the **Paste** button in the **Clipboard** group.

Data pasted into a document from Excel or Access is displayed in a Word table, and can be edited and manipulated using the table-handling features in Word (see Chapter 6).

12.3   Working with Excel data

If the data or chart you require already exists in an Excel spreadsheet, you can copy and paste it into your Word document, or copy the data in with a link to the original data, or embed the data in your document.

Linking data

You can copy data with a link to the original in Excel. A representation of the data is displayed in Word, but the actual data is held and updated in Excel. This is useful when file size is a consideration, or when it is important that the data in Word is kept in line with the data in Excel.

To link the data that you paste from Excel to the source file, follow the Copy and Paste routine above, then click the **Paste Options** button and choose a Link option.

○ Keep Source Formatting
○ Match Destination Table Style
○ Paste as Picture
○ Keep Text Only
○ Keep Source Formatting and Link to Excel
◉ Match Destination Table Style and Link to Excel

By default, the updating option for linked objects is set to Automatic. This means that the file in Word is updated each time you open it, or each time the source data in Excel is updated when the destination file in Word is open. You can edit the linking and updating options in the Links dialog box.

1 Click the Microsoft Office button, choose **Prepare** and then **Edit Links to Files**.

2 Specify the Links options.

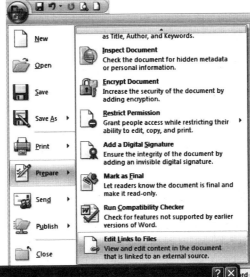

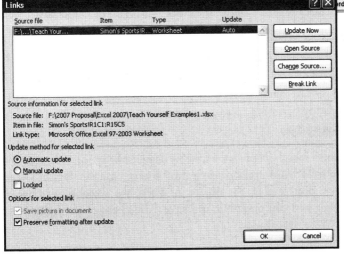

- You can opt to manually update the linked data, and then use **Update now** to update the data when you choose, or you can permanently break the link between the files.

3 Click **OK**.

- To update a linked object at any time, right-click on it and choose **Update Link**.

Embedded data

When you embed existing data, a copy of it is held in the Word document. You can embed the data with or without a link to the original.

To embed existing Excel data into your Word document use Copy and Paste Special.

1 Open the workbook that contains the data or chart.

2 Select the data or chart and click the **Copy** tool.

3 Switch to the Word document you want to paste into.

4 Place the insertion point where you want the object to go.

5 Click the arrow under the **Paste** button in the **Clipboard** group and choose **Paste Special...**

6 Select the **Paste Link** button if you want a link to the original data.

7 Choose **Microsoft Office Excel Worksheet Object** from the **As:** list

8 Click **OK**.

If you embed an object with the Paste link option selected, the data in Word is updated each time you update the data in Excel. If you double-click the object in Word, the Excel file is opened so that you can update it and save. The changes are reflected in the Word document.

Embedded data without a link

If you choose Paste: rather than the Paste link option at the Paste Special dialog box, you can edit the data in Word by double-clicking on the object. All the Excel tools and menus are displayed so that you can work on the embedded data, but the changes are not reflected in the original Excel file.

If you want an Excel spreadsheet in a Word document, but don't need it for any other purpose, you can use Insert Excel Spreadsheet. A sheet can be created and edited using Excel functions. One inserted in this way is an embedded object.

To insert an Excel spreadsheet:

1 Place the insertion point where you want the worksheet.

2 Click the arrow under the **Table** button in the **Tables** group on the **Insert** tab.

3 Choose **Excel Spreadsheet**.

♦ This creates an embedded spreadsheet, with the toolbars and menus of Excel displayed.

	A	B	C	D	E	F
1		January	February	March	April	Total
2	Ann	130	200	300	250	880
3	Bill	250	150	100	240	740
4	Cara	175	250	200	190	815
5	Dawn	220	240	180	220	860
6	Total	775	840	780	900	3295

Sheet1

4 Set up the spreadsheet using Excel's tools and menus.

5 Resize the spreadsheet if necessary.

6 Click anywhere outside the spreadsheet area when you've finished.

7 To return to Excel to edit the spreadsheet, double-click on it.

12.4 Charts

If you want a chart in Word, and it isn't already set up in Excel, you can create the chart from within Word. You will find that you have access to all of the charting power of Excel – provided you have it installed on your computer. When using this, a chart appears with its associated data in a table called a *datasheet*. You can then type your data into the datasheet, or import it from a text file, or paste it from another program to the datasheet.

* If you do not have Excel 2007, you can create charts using Microsoft Graph, one of the Office Tools supplied with Word. Its charting routines are very similar to those of Excel. Use the online Help as necessary if you are using Graph.

Some of the main features are discussed here. If you have used charting in Excel or PowerPoint you will find that the feature works exactly the same in Word.

To create a chart:

1 Click the **Chart** button in the **Illustrations** group.

2 Select the chart type you want to create in the left pane of the **Create Chart** dialog box.

3 Choose a subtype from the right pane in the dialog box.

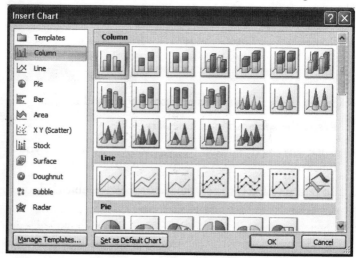

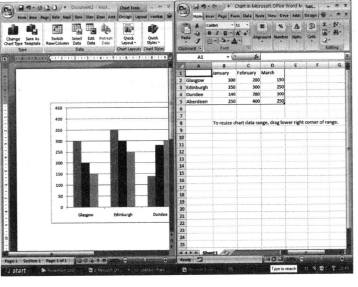

4 Click **OK**.

• Sample chart data is displayed in an Excel window, side-by-side with your document.

5 Edit the contents on the Excel worksheet as required.

6 Close Excel when you have entered your data. Your chart will be displayed.

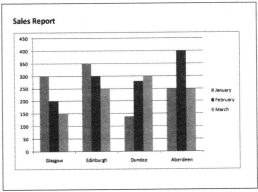

• When you create a chart in this way its data is embedded in the Word file, but you input and edit the data using Excel.

Resize, move and delete charts

If you want to move, resize or delete a chart that is an object in a document, you must select the chart first.

To resize the chart:

1 Select the chart.

2 Point to one of the handles in the corner or along the edge of the chart – the pointer changes to a 2-headed arrow when it is in a suitable place.

3 Click and drag to resize the chart.

To move the chart:

1 Select the chart.

2 Point to an edge of the chart (not a handle) – the pointer changes to a 4-headed arrow when it is in a suitable place.

3 Drag and drop the chart in its new location.

To delete the chart:

♦ Select the chart and press [Delete].

When the chart is selected the Chart Tools appear on the Ribbon. This has three tabs: Design, Layout and Format.

♦ If you click outside the Chart area, the Chart Tools disappear. Click within the Chart area again and they reappear.

Editing source data

If you need to edit the source data (that contained on the Excel worksheet), click the Edit Data button in the Data group. The worksheet will be displayed, and you can edit the data as required.

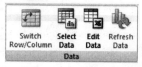

Chart type

If your chart doesn't look the way you want, you can change it to a different chart type.

To change the chart type:

1 Click the **Change Chart Type** button in the **Type** group on the **Design** tab.

2 Select the type and subtype required.

3 Click **OK**.

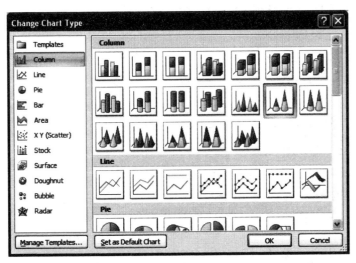

Chart styles and layouts

There are a variety of chart styles and layouts that you can use to enable you to quickly adjust and format your chart.

The **chart styles** give you access to a wide range of carefully colour-coordinated options that can be applied to your chart.

To change the chart style:

1 Select your chart.

2 Scroll through the **Chart Style** options on the **Design** tab of the **Chart** tools.

More

Or

- Click the **More** button at the bottom right of the Chart Style group to display all the Chart styles available.

3 Select the one you want to use.

The **chart layout** affects the inclusion and positioning of objects like the chart heading, legend, data table, axis labels, etc.

The quickest way to include or exclude objects from your chart is to use one of the predefined chart layouts.

1 Select your chart.

2 Scroll through the **Chart Layout** options on the **Design** tab of the **Chart** tools.

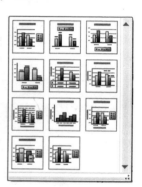

Or

- Click the **More** button at the bottom right of the **Chart Layout** group to display all the layout options.

3 Select the one you want to use.

To delete a chart object:

1 Right click on it.

2 Select **Delete** from the menu.

	Delete
	Reset to Match Style
A	Font...
	Change Chart Type...
	Edit Data...
	3-D Rotation...
	Format Legend...

To format a chart object:

1 Right-click on the object.

2 Left-click on the **Format Chart Area/Title/Series...** option (depending on what you right-click on).

3 Explore the dialog box, selecting the options required.

4 Click **OK**.

Chart titles and axis labels

If you select a layout with a chart title and/or axis labels, the areas are text boxes, and initially they contain default text – 'Chart Title' in the title area and 'Axis Title' along each axis.

To replace the default text with your own:

1 Click once on the label to select it.

2 Click a second time to place the insertion point in it.

3 Delete the default text and type in your label.

4 Click outside the title or label area – anywhere on your chart.

Chart Layout options

You can switch individual objects on and off using the buttons in the Labels, Axes and Background groups of the Layout tab, or reposition objects by applying one of the standard layouts.

* The Labels group includes the Chart Headings, Axis Titles, Legend, Data Labels and Data Table.

* The Axes group includes the Axes and the Gridlines.

* The Background group includes the Plot Area (on a 2-D chart), Chart Wall, Chart Floor and 3-D View (on a 3-D chart).

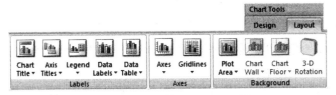

To display or reposition an object:

1 Click the object's button.

2 Select the required position.

To remove an object:

1 Click the object's button.

2 Select **None**.

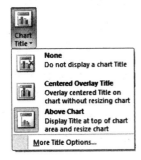

To adjust the format of an object:

1 Click the object's button.

2 Select **More Options...** and explore the dialog box.

3 Select the options required and click **OK**.

Some objects have many more options than others. Walls, floors and plot areas have fill colours and effects. Lines have styles, colours and widths. Explore and experiment – some options will appeal to you, others will not. Don't overdo things! The purpose of your chart is to clearly and effectively present your data – not to demonstrate every chart formatting option!

12.5 Word and PowerPoint

You can generate a Word document from a PowerPoint presentation. This feature gives you additional options for creating notes pages and handouts from your PowerPoint presentation file.

1 In PowerPoint, open the presentation.

2 Click the Microsoft Office button and choose **Publish**, then **Create Handouts in Microsoft Office Word**.

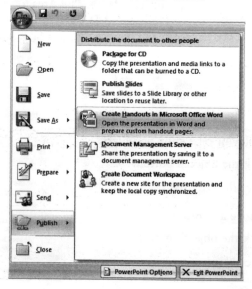

3 Choose a page layout in the dialog box.

4 Select **Paste** or **Paste link**.

5 Click **OK**.

A new document will be created in Word. You can save and/or print the document as required.

If you Paste link, your Word document will automatically update when the PowerPoint presentation is edited and saved.

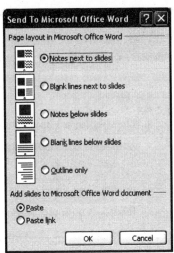

12.6 Word and Access

You can copy and paste from an Access table in the same way as you can from an Excel worksheet. You can also use an Access table or query as a data source in a mail merge (see Chapter 9).

To use an Access table or query as a data source in mail merge:

1 In Word, create or open your main document.

2 Click **Select Recipients** in the **Start Mail Merge** group.

3 Locate the database that you want to link to.

4 Open the database.

5 Select the table or query you want to link to.

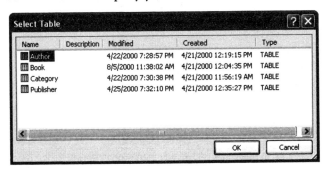

6 Click **OK**.

You can also link to an Excel worksheet in the same way, selecting any sheet or named range as your data source.

Summary

In this chapter we have discussed:

- Linking and embedding
- Copy and paste
- Linking and embedding existing Excel data
- Inserting an Excel worksheet into a Word document
- Creating charts in documents
- Creating a Word document from a presentation
- Using an Access table or query in a Word mail merge.

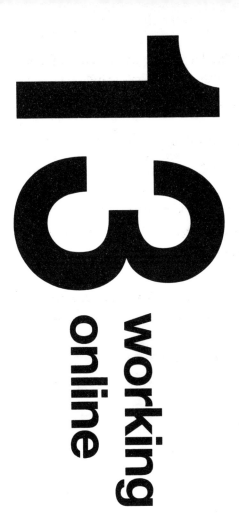

13 working online

In this chapter you will learn:

- how to send an e-mail from Word
- how to post a blog entry from Word
- how to use the Research tool

13.1 E-mail

Provided you have a modem, communications software and an Internet service provider, you can e-mail your Word document to anywhere in the world. E-mail is usually very fast – sometimes your message will be delivered almost instantly, and it rarely takes more than an hour.

You can create a document and send it by e-mail from within Word. (You can also, of course, send an existing document from within Word, or attach one to an e-mail message in your e-mail application.)

To create a new e-mail within Word:

1 Create a new document or open an existing one.

2 Enter and edit your text as necessary.

3 Click the Microsoft Office button, choose **Send**, then **E-mail**.

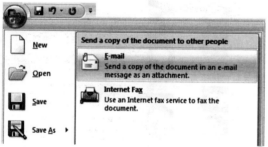

4 Your message becomes an attachment in your e-mail.

5 Complete the **To...**, **Cc...** and **Subject** fields as required.

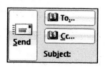

6 Click **Send**.

13.2 To publish to a blog

You must have a blog account set up before you can use this feature. If you want a blog, check out the online Help and follow the prompts from Word if necessary.

A blog, or Web log, is a website that you can add your own content to, updating it with new entries on a regular basis. There are several blog providers that allow you to post an entry directly from Word. You publish the content of your document to your blog and it appears as an entry on your site. Most blogs allow you to publish a variety of media – text, photos, videos, audio, etc. Some blogs provide information and commentary on a particular subject, e.g. local news or politics. Others are used as social spaces where you can publish your diary, leave information for your friends, share photographs, etc.

To create a blog post from an existing document:

1 Create or open the document you want to post.

2 Enter and edit your text.

3 Click the Microsoft Office button and choose **Publish**, then **Blog**.

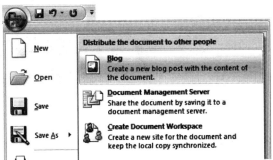

◆ Your document is displayed in Web Layout view, and the **Blog Post** tab appears on the Ribbon.

4 Give your blog a title.

5 Insert a category if you wish.

6 Make any final adjustments to your entry.

7 Publish it.

Don't forget to visit your blog to check out your posting!

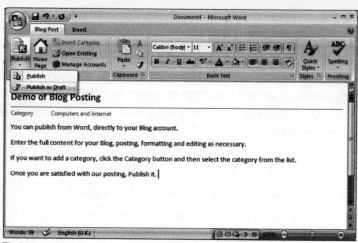

The blog content can be prepared and published from within Word.

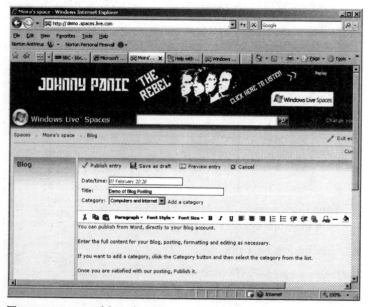

To create a new blog document:

1 Click the Microsoft Office button and choose **New**.

2 In the **Blank and Recent** category, click **New Blog Post**.

3 Click **Create**, then complete and publish as above.

13.3 Research

If you write reports and articles where you need to research your details, you can use the Research feature and work from within Word itself. The feature enables you to quickly locate reference information on your computer or online without leaving Word. The research options include a thesaurus, translation tools and access to online reference sites. It's easy to use and you can customize its settings to suit your own research needs.

To start your research:

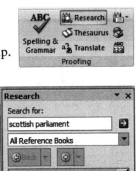

1 Display the **Review** tab.

2 Click **Research** in the Proofing group.

3 Type in the word/phrase you that you want to research.

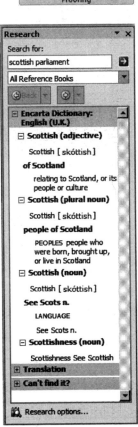

4 Choose the research places from the reference books and sites available.

5 Click [→].

• The results of your search will be displayed in the Research panel.

6 Scroll through the results and read any articles that may be relevant.

To add reference sites to your research options:

1 Click **Research options...** at the bottom of the Research panel.

2 Update the options as required.

3 Click **OK**.

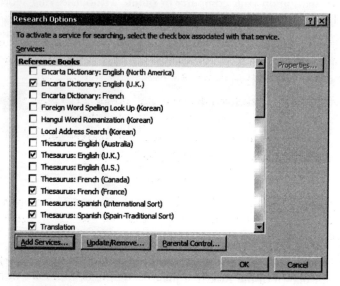

Summary

This chapter has looked at some ways of integrating Word with the Internet. We have discussed:

* Sending e-mails directly from Word

* Posting an entry to a blog

* Using the research feature.

Bitten by the blog bug?

If you would like to learn more about blogging and set up your own interactive blog, try *Teach Yourself Blogging*.

taking it further

If you've mastered half of what's in this book, you are well on the way to becoming a proficient Word user. If you are getting to grips with most of it, you are doing very well indeed.

You'll find lots of information on Word on the Internet, in addition to the Microsoft Help pages. Try these sites:

http://www.microsoft.com/en-gb/word/default.asp

http://office.microsoft.com/en-gb/help

http://support.microsoft.com/search/

You could also search the Web for sites that provide information on Word. Enter "Microsoft Word" into a search engine. You should come up with several sites worth a look.

If you would like to join a course to consolidate your skills, try your local college, or search the Internet for online courses. Good Word skills are useful on many levels – personal, educational and vocational. Now that you have improved your Word skills, why not try for certification? The challenge of an exam can be fun, and a recognized certificate may improve your job prospects. There are a number of different bodies that you could consider.

You may want to consider MOS (Microsoft Office Specialist) exams or ECDL (European Computer Driving Licence – basic or advanced) certification. Or, if you feel more ambitious, how about other Microsoft Certified Professional exams?

For information on MOS certification, visit:

http://www.microsoft.com/learning/mcp/officespecialist/default.mspx

or for information on ECDL, visit:

http://www.ecdl.co.uk

index

| teach yourself | **Windows Vista** |
| | mac bride |

- Are you new to Windows Vista?
- Do you use Windows Vista at home or in the office?
- Do you need to brush up your skills?

Windows Vista explains all of the key aspects of this application from the user's angle, including running programs and managing files, getting online, managing your email, maintaining your system, configuring printers, customizing your system, getting help and using accessories. Written for the new user at home or in the office, it covers all the key features of Windows Vista and helps the reader to maximize his/her use of the system with confidence.

Mac Bride is a successful author of computing and other books who brings 20 years of teaching experience to his writing.